Dreaming a way (of) Life

Since his debut in the 1980s, Lewis Klahr has built a mesmerizing and influential body of work, establishing himself as one of the foremost collage animators—or, as he prefers, a "re-animator." His films explore themes of identity (*Altair*), childhood (*The Pharaoh's Belt*), sexuality (*Pony Glass*, *Downs Are Feminine*), memory (*False Aging*, *Daylight Moon*, *Engram Sepals*), Greek mythology (*Lethe*, *Helen of T*, *66*), and capitalism (*Circumstantial Pleasures*). These philosophical explorations are often veiled behind the familiar veneer of mid-20th-century American pop culture—drawing inspiration from film noir, melodrama, crime films, popular music, and comic books.

Working with an eclectic mix of found imagery—including magazine ads, home movies, contact sheets, pornography, and comic books—along with layered soundscapes, Klahr's characters drift through fragmented times and spaces, searching for connection and an elusive sense of self.

Despite the allure of vivid pop culture references, Klahr's films resist easy interpretation. His elliptical, dream-like narratives challenge viewers, creating spaces where meaning remains fluid and unresolved. Yet this ambiguity is intentional—Klahr embraces the uncertainty between his work and its audience, inviting exploration over resolution.

In *Dreaming a way (of) Life: The Films of Lewis Klahr*, award-winning writer **Chris Robinson** (*The Animation Pimp*, *Unsung Heroes of Animation*, *Earmarked for Collision*) offers the first full-length study of this prolific and influential collage animator. Through insightful analysis, Robinson unveils the depth and complexity of Klahr's artistic vision, guiding readers into the magic and mystery of his cinematic universe.

Key Features:

- First in-depth study of the work of American collage artist, Lewis Klahr
- Mixed biography with a philosophically influenced approach to the major themes of Klahr's work
- Introduction of important experimental and independent animation figure that shows readers animation beyond typical industry fare

Focus Animation

The Focus Animation Series aims to provide unique, accessible content that may not otherwise be published. We allow researchers, academics, and professionals the ability to quickly publish high impact, current literature in the field of animation for a global audience. This series is a fine complement to the existing, robust animation titles available through CRC Press/Focal Press.

Series Editor Chris Robinson is the Artistic Director of the Ottawa International Animation Festival (OIAF) and is a well-known figure in the animated film world. We welcome any submissions to help grow the wonderful content we are striving to provide to the animation community.

A Moving Subject
Giannalberto Bendazzi;

Wharfie Animator: Harry Reade, The Sydney Waterfront, and the Cuban Revolution
Max Bannah;

Mad Eyed Misfits: Writings on Indie Animation
Chris Robinson;

Life in Death: My Animated Films 1976–2020
Dennis Tupicoff;

Chinese Animated Film and Ideology, 1940s–1970s: Fighting Puppets
Olga Bobrowska;

Nordic Animation Balancing the East and the West
Liisa Vähäkylä;

Classic Chinese Animated Film and Ideology: Tradition, Innovation, and Interculturality
Olga Bobrowska;

Cheer and Loathing: Scattered Ramblings on Indie Animation
Chris Robinson;

Michel Ocelot: A World of Animated Images
Laura Buono;

Dreaming a way (of) Life: The Films of Lewis Klahr
Chris Robinson;

For more information about this series, please visit: https://www.routledge.com/Focus-Animation/book-series/CRCFOCUSANI

Dreaming a way (of) Life

The Films of Lewis Klahr

Chris Robinson

CRC Press is an imprint of the
Taylor & Francis Group, an **informa** business

First edition published 2025
by CRC Press
2385 NW Executive Center Drive, Suite 320, Boca Raton FL 33431

and by CRC Press
4 Park Square, Milton Park, Abingdon, Oxon, OX14 4RN

CRC Press is an imprint of Taylor & Francis Group, LLC

Library of Congress Cataloging-in-Publication Data
Names: Robinson, Chris, 1967– author.
Title: Dreaming a way (of) life : the films of Lewis Klahr / Chris Robinson.
Description: First edition. | Boca Raton, FL : CRC Press, 2025. | Series: Focus animation | Includes bibliographical references, filmography, and index. | Identifiers: LCCN 2024051453 (print) | LCCN 2024051454 (ebook) | ISBN 9781032537191 (hbk) | ISBN 9781032547299 (pbk) | ISBN 9781003427223 (ebk)
Subjects: LCSH: Klahr, Lewis—Criticism and interpretation. | Cutout animation films—History and criticism. | Animators—United States—Biography
Classification: LCC NC1766.U52 K5957 2025 (print) | LCC NC1766.U52 (ebook) | DDC 791.43/34092 [B]—dc23/eng/20241229
LC record available at https://lccn.loc.gov/2024051453
LC ebook record available at https://lccn.loc.gov/2024051454

ISBN: 9781032537191 (hbk)
ISBN: 9781032547299 (pbk)
ISBN: 9781003427223 (ebk)

DOI: 10.1201/9781003427223

Typeset in Times LT
by codeMantra

For Product Safety Concerns and Information please contact our EU representative: GPSR@taylorandfrancis.com.

Taylor & Francis Verlag GmbH, Kaufingerstraße 24, 80331 München, Germany.

"But these memories drifted away like bubbles of soap or fragments of a dream that vanished on waking."

Patrick Modiano, *So You Don't Get Lost in The Neighborhood*

"Was I bored? No, I wasn't fuckin' bored. I'm never bored. That's the trouble with everybody – you're all so bored. You've had nature explained to you, and you're bored with it. You've had the living body explained to you, and you're bored with it. You've had the universe explained to you, and you're bored with it. So now you just want cheap thrills and like plenty of 'em, and it don't matter how tawdry or vacuous they are as long as it's new, as long as it's new, as long as it flashes and fucking bleeps in forty different colours."

Mike Leigh, *Naked*

For Lightning Girl

Contents

Blissful Melancholy: Introduction and Acknowledgements

It's Robert Pollard's fault. It always is.

"Who?" you ask.

Robert Pollard is an American musician and collage artist, best known as the frontman of the band Guided by Voices. While reading a book about one of the band's albums, I stumbled upon a chapter featuring an interview with collage animator Lewis Klahr. The name sounded familiar—likely from an animation DVD compilation called *Anxious Animation*—but I didn't know much about him. Still, if Klahr was connected to Pollard, I felt compelled to dig deeper.

Since the 1980s, Lewis Klahr has created a mesmerizing and prolific body of work, establishing himself as one of the most influential collage animators of our time (though he prefers the term "re-animator"). His films construct complex, layered worlds that grapple with themes of identity (*Altair*), childhood (*The Pharaoh's Belt*), sexuality (*Pony Glass, Downs Are Feminine*), time (*False Aging, Daylight Moon, Engram Sepals*), mythology (*Lethe, Helen of T, 66*), and capitalism (*Circumstantial Pleasures, Engram Sepals*). These themes often lie hidden beneath the inviting façade of mid-20th-century American pop culture, drawing inspiration from film noir, melodrama, crime films, popular music, and comic books.

Klahr's films serenade us like sirens. We're lured in by the technicolor veneer of pop culture, often underscored by the melancholic sounds of musicians like Julie London, Frank Sinatra, Scott Walker, Lana Del Rey, Tobin Sprout, and The Velvet Underground. But, once fully immersed, we find ourselves adrift. Moments we thought we could grasp dissolve almost instantly, replaced by fleeting, elusive scenes. His films ache with alienation, disconnection, and longing, suspended in a liminal space between dream, mass media, and memory. Watching his work is akin to recalling a dream—fragments of beauty from an impossible puzzle.

It's tempting to view his films as nostalgic tributes to mid-century America, but that's only part of the picture. These works exist in a perpetual present, flickering in and out like memories or dreams—there one moment, gone the next. Before, we can process what we've witnessed, it slips away, much like trying to recount a dream before it fades. Klahr's films evoke emotions rather than provide concrete answers, leaving viewers to navigate their own interpretations.

Though Klahr sets the course, we, the viewers, determine where it leads. The beacons and markers he lays out are mere suggestions—the ultimate destination is left to us. Collage, by its nature, needs capitalism, or at least consumerism. It thrives on the detritus of our cultural landscape—magazines, ads, comic books, and films—to construct its worlds.

Klahr's work seduces with a promise of beauty and comfort, only to pull the rug out from beneath us. We're left to piece things together on our own. His films, for all their candy-colored allure, resist easy interpretation. Their elliptical narratives, much like dreams, defy clear logic or structure. There's no fixed center, only a complex interplay between the personal and the public, memory and advertising.

His characters, composed of found images—magazine ads, home movies, contact sheets, porn, comic books—drift through disconnected times and spaces, craving connection and a sense of self that remains just out of reach, even when it seems tantalizingly close.

This book is meant as a modest introduction to Klahr's often-overlooked and complex body of work, particularly within the animation world. Klahr himself rejects the label of animator, preferring to see himself as a "re-animator"—though technically, the word "animator" is still in there.

Like Klahr, I approach projects with only a vague plan, relying on intuition as I move forward. Writing, for me, is a process of discovery, and it's only by the end of the journey that I understand my true thoughts on the subject.

In this book, I aim to explore what I see as the key elements of Klahr's work—memory, myth, love, time, aging, and music. While I've divided the chapters by theme, Klahr's films often weave these concerns together in intricate and unexpected ways. Compartmentalization is sometimes necessary to unravel these overlapping ideas, but the richness of Klahr's work always transcends such boundaries.

Before diving in, I've included a selection of interviews I conducted with Klahr in 2023 and 2024 to provide additional insight into his process.

First and foremost, I extend my deepest thanks to Lewis Klahr for his generosity, support, and insight.

Honor Roll: Igor Prassel, Yiorgos Tsangaris, Anastasyia Verlinska, Vera Duffy, Barbara Duffy, Magdalena Zira, Kelly Sears, Janie Geiser, Gerben Schermer, Jelena Popović, Robert Pollard, Kelly Neall, Harry Neall, Jarvis Neall, my colleagues at the Ottawa International Animation Festival, and the many sharp minds who have observed and interpreted Klahr's work, in particular, Tom Gunning, Chris Stults.

About the Author

Chris Robinson is a Canadian writer and the Artistic Director of the Ottawa International Animation Festival (OIAF). A leading figure in the animation world, Robinson has received several prestigious honors, including the **Animafest Zagreb Award for Outstanding Contribution to Animation Studies** (2020) and the **Prix René Jodoin** (2022) for his contributions to Canadian animation. Widely regarded as "one of the most stylistically original and provocative experts in the history of animation," Robinson's influence extends across writing, curation, and film.

Robinson first garnered attention through his eclectic and influential magazine column, *The Animation Pimp*, which was later adapted into a book of the same name. Beyond his contributions as a critic and historian, Robinson co-wrote the award-winning animated short *Lipsett Diaries* (2010), directed by Theodore Ushev. More recently, he collaborated with German artist Andreas Hykade on an illustrated novel titled *My Balls Are Killing Me.*

1 Meet the Star: A Conversation with Lewis Klahr

Lewis Klahr

DOI: 10.1201/9781003427223-1

EARLY YEARS

How did you stumble upon collage?

I first experienced collage most directly with a painting that my mother, who was an interior decorator, bought by the side of the road in upstate New York near a bungalow colony my family summered at in the late 1950s and early 1960s. This painting was a cityscape with storefronts that were representational but partially abstract with newspaper collaged in, including an ad for an 8mm movie projector, which now, ironically, feels prophetic of my use of Super 8. I grew up with this painting and for a long time really hated it—I thought it was ugly and *not the way a picture should look*. But over the years and decades, as my taste enlarged and matured, the painting's aesthetic seeped into me. Gradually, I came to love it. Today it hangs in my studio as a continual inspiration and something I'm trying to figure out how to make my version of as a film.

When did you begin seeing art more seriously?

Early in college, one of the first things I saw was Robert Rauschenberg's silkscreen paintings. I immediately loved the way he had montaged newspaper imagery of JFK, astronauts, New York City, and baseball star Mickey Mantle into his compositions. For Rauschenberg, when he made these screen-printed collages, this imagery was current and completely present tense. But, for me, looking at them more than a decade later in the mid-1970s, they were my early childhood. This gave me an immediate connection and access to understanding those works. But seeing Rauschenberg's work didn't make me want to do collage. I couldn't draw and didn't conceive of myself as a potential visual artist. At that point, I wanted to be a writer.

These experiences I'm describing were experiences that, in retrospect, now seem more important than they seemed at the time.

They're like seeds that were planted. So, how did cinema and cutout animation enter the picture?

Yeah, like seeds that sprouted because in January 1977 I saw a history of the American avant-garde cinema that the Whitney Museum and NYU had put together that toured colleges. It was two nights a week with a lecturer at SUNY at Purchase, the college I was on a year's leave of absence from. Included was Larry Jordan's *Our Lady of the Sphere*. (I might have seen Stan VanDerBeek's Science Friction too.) I immediately felt that collaging cutouts was what I wanted to do and something I could do. Of course, I'd seen cutout animation before in Monty Python and Yellow Submarine and liked both. But seeing Our Lady of the Sphere was different—as was seeing experimental film at that point—both felt empowering and like ways of working that were accessible to me. Unlike Hollywood filmmaking, experimental

The Pharoah's Belt

filmmaking was like being a poet, painter, or musician—a practice one could perform daily and in domestic settings and without a large budget.

But before I committed myself fully to doing cutout animation, I wanted to learn about other kinds of experimental filmmaking. I wanted to take my time and build up to using cutouts. I didn't want to waste my use of cutouts on my immaturity as a filmmaker. So, I started to shoot and edit live-action experimental S8 films, at first renting equipment from The Millenium Film Co-op in the East Village before eventually purchasing my own.

By June of 1977, I had my first film finished. The next September, I returned to college at SUNY at Buffalo. I studied with Paul Sharits, who was big on students making scores for films, and I made my first single-frame film from a score I composed with one of my best friends, Josh Rosen, who was a jazz pianist. Josh taught me about additive rhythms, and I made an edited, in the camera portrait of a block of Buffalo houses that had different colors and shapes that interested me. To follow the score, I had to walk up and down the street between the different houses, set up my Super 8 camera, and shoot the required frames before resetting the camera for my next shot. The score also specified the time of day I needed to shoot. My next single frame, edited in the camera project, was loose and spontaneous—a diary film I made from June to early August 1978 on a single 50-foot roll of S8. These films began my exploration of single framing.

Another reason I wanted to put off doing cutout animation was that I knew I needed to amass a stockpile of source materials to collage from. This of course meant finding and saving source materials, something I understood was going to take time. I had always saved certain things, but not for any artistic purpose. In my "Nimbus Films Trilogy" (2010), for instance, there's a holiday greeting card my parents received of a New York cityscape that's on reflective paper (depending on how the light hits it, the sky and buildings dramatically change color), which I saved from when I was 12 years old. Why did I keep it? I don't know; I guess I thought it looked "cool." It only took me 30 years to find a film to use it in. But as I discovered, that's an important part of doing collage—waiting patiently for the right context to use saved materials in.

The first source material I consciously saved with the thought of using for cutout animation was my family's 1956 World Book Encyclopedia. My parents wanted to donate it to charity, but I said, No, I need that for my filmmaking. My dad looked at me like I was crazy and said something to the effect of how I was denying some kid a chance to have this useful educational resource. However, I stood my ground, and my parents honored my request and stored the encyclopedia. I did make great use of that encyclopedia—essential images in my early cutout animation *Deep Fishtank Birding,* and later, my epic depiction of my childhood, *The Pharoah's Belt*, came out of those volumes: birds, swimmers, divers, train conductors, and on and on to the present day, where I still find myself plucking useful images from it.

The Pharoah's Belt

I knew I was onto something with that mid-20th-century imagery. Jordan primarily uses Victorian-era or early 20th-century cutouts. It was not only challenging to find those images, but they were expensive to purchase. Plus, it felt like Jordan owned that era. You couldn't use it without being compared to him, and I hadn't even seen Joseph Cornell's collage boxes, Max Ernst's collage novels, or Harry Smith's *Heaven and Earth Magic* Feature yet, which also used that imagery! But this wasn't much of an obstacle really, since what I was attracted to was images from my own lifetime, or somewhat before, that had been contemporary in my parent's lives. I was interested in the way these gave me access to an imagination of the past, a kind of time travel. Just like I experienced with the Rauschenberg newspaper images, there was a sense of both personal and American cultural history.

Were you always a collector, or did that come later?

It came later. I believe most people have collecting impulses, and for me, this manifested first through things like baseball cards and, then, as a teenager, with record collecting. When I was around eight or nine, my maternal grandfather came to visit and said he had a special present for me. He worked in the office of a paper company and had international correspondence from around the world. So, he gifted me all these stamped envelopes. I couldn't hide my disappointment. My nine-year-old brain was thinking, *What, no toy? What kind of special present is this? What can I do with a bunch of stamps?*

Collage artists are a bit like hoarders, but they're also very different—just as they are different from archivists. While hoarders and archivists want to protect and preserve what they save, as a collage artist, I'm the exact opposite. I'm interested in the use value of my source materials, which usually means destroying the source they're lifted from.

My grandfather and step-grandmother were definitely hoarders. In the late 1980s, after they had passed, my mother inherited their house in Pittsfield, Massachusetts. (It was then that I discovered hoarding or collecting is a bit of genetic inheritance for me.) Preparing the house for sale required cleaning out everything my grandparents had saved. There was even a room we didn't know existed because so much stuff was piled up in front of it! Eventually, I found *Playboy* #1 buried in that hidden room. When I researched its value, I found out there were a lot of copies of *Playboy* #1 because so many people had saved it. The issue that was really valuable was *Playboy* #2, which sold far fewer copies, and nobody saved—LOL.

It took my mother, father, sisters, and me many different weekend trips to clear out the house. But I immediately knew I needed to sift through everything to see what I could use to build my storehouse of collected images. This slowed the cleanout process considerably, but what I found were books, magazines, newspapers, photos, letters, labels, bottles, buttons, objects, and fabrics that had fantastic value for my work. To acquire such a huge amount of source material in antique and thrift stores, I would have had to spend thousands and thousands of dollars. So, ironically, my grandfather ended up giving me the greatest inheritance I could have ever wanted. And included in my bequest were lots more of those envelopes with international stamps like the ones he'd tried—and failed—to interest me in when I was nine!

At the time, I lived and worked in a small one-bedroom apartment in the East Village on Avenue B. I had to figure out how to store everything, so I had a loft bed built to put my source materials underneath. Most of my source materials were in varying degrees of decay, and a lot of it was moldy. When I was making my film *The Organ Minder's Gronkey* (1990), a version of the sci-fi, post-nuclear apocalypse survivor films that had terrified and fascinated me as a kid, I started to feel sick every day. For a couple of weeks, I believed I was having some kind of psychosomatic reaction analogous to radiation poisoning, and I thought—I better hurry up and finish this film before it kills me! Finally, I realized it was just an allergic reaction to the mold. I wrapped my source materials in a large plastic tarp, and my illness ended.

COLLAGE AS ART

Hi-Fi Cadets

What draws you to collage as a technique as opposed to just shooting something live or using puppets or whatever?

As curator Chris Stults wrote about my body of work, "Klahr's great subject is time." Collage is special to me because of how time-centric it is. The timestamp of a found image offers me a portal for time travel. Collage is also a reactive form—jumpstarting my creative process by providing something already created to respond to and engage with. While this isn't unique to collage, I believe collage emphasizes and foregrounds this reality to a higher degree than most other forms.

Another important factor that drew me to collage was that I couldn't draw. Collage allowed me to create visual and moving image art using the skill set I did have—my sense of color, texture, mise en scène, and juxtaposition. Working with cutouts leveraged what is perhaps my main talent with collage: an ability to empathetically project myself into appropriated images and sequence them in a way that grants them a new or second life through recontextualization. This is what I mean when I say I'm less an animator than a re-animator.

I made found footage films for several years before switching to cutout animation. My media autobiography *Picture Books for Adults* (1983–1985) is a good example. But I wasn't ultimately satisfied with the found footage. I wanted more control and freedom, which is why I switched to cutouts. In the second half of 1987, when working with cutouts became my main practice, I immediately felt at home. I'd found my voice. This was so emotionally overwhelming for me that I literally had to stop shooting *For the Rest of Your Natural Life* (1988)—the first film I worked on in my *Tales of the Forgotten Future* series—for several weeks. It felt so pleasurable it actually hurt.

I originally wanted to be a Hollywood narrative filmmaker, but I knew I was ill-suited for that pursuit. Plus, I wanted to do something I could engage in every day, which working in the domestic, small-scale production of cutout animation made possible. I could miniaturize the kinds of events that occur in narrative movies. I could make my own versions of classic Hollywood films. I had my own movie studio backlot on an 8″ × 11″ set. And because my films didn't cost much to make, I had the freedom to create the films I wanted to and tell the poetic and elliptical subjective narratives I was passionate about. For me, cutout animation was an extension of what I was used to doing as a child—playing with toy soldiers to tell myself fictional stories. I was creating an adult version of that childhood playground through the cutouts.

How do you navigate the inherent limitations of collage art, where you're often constrained by the availability of existing materials, and how do you turn these constraints into creative possibilities?

I've usually found that limitation was good for my art and early on in my single-frame collage films, I decided to double down on it. Collage because of scarcity of source materials tends to foreground limitation anyway. Things like Photoshop didn't interest me as workarounds because I found the effect of limitation had more impact and aesthetic fascination for me. I've always been interested in pulling my audience in and out of the fictive illusions I was creating. I wanted my audience to engage with many different states of viewership from complete immersion and investment in my source materials to dislocation where they would fall out of the fictive universe I was creating and think about the fact that they were watching a film.

Something else that separates you from collage artists, like Terry Gilliam or Stan Vanderbeek, is that you don't satirize the material

Yes. I never feel above my material. I have a sense of humor, but it doesn't distance itself as much as satire does and humor is rarely my primary form of address which it is for Gilliam. In the 1980s, when I started to work with collage, I saw my contemporaries sticking in the ironic knife and critically twisting 1950s, 1960s, and 1970s imagery. That always felt like too easy a target to me. Irony also felt like too easy a way out—I wanted to acknowledge that I'm from and belong to the society—often middle class—the imagery I use is from. I wanted to engage with a broader spectrum of emotions than irony afforded. Distance interests me but more in the philosophical way I describe above.

Another tendency that I've seen with collage (even collage art) is the constant criticism of advertising, consumerism, and capitalism. And of course, they should all be critiqued, but I also found it strange that the collage artist is sort of biting the hand that feeds. You can't make these collage works without the very thing you're criticizing

Exactly. I want to self-implicate. I have my thoughts about the capitalist system and harsh criticisms of it, but I also live inside and am a part of it. There's this kind of push and pull between criticizing and enjoying and appreciating. What I came to grips with and wanted to describe was that it had created my consciousness in different ways. That was undeniable and not all of it was negative.

Nimbus Trilogy

What are your thoughts on questions of authenticity, originality, and copyright within the collage context?

I didn't think about those issues much when I started collaging but over time, their depth opened up. Authenticity first manifested for me in the 1980s and 1990s in relation to photocopying. Usually, this involved there being two images on the two sides of a page of my source materials that overlapped, which required me to pick which image to cutout. This became a challenging decision when I wanted to have both. Photocopying of course altered the aura of my source materials both in terms of paper quality and color. Also, it was important whether or not the "copy" conveyed that it was a copy. This could create discontinuities I didn't want or think had aesthetic value for the specific film I was creating. Most of the time, I found myself prioritizing the aura of my original sources, and using copies as infrequently as possible.

When I first became a collage filmmaker I accepted what I perceived to be the standard viewpoint about originality and collage: that it was acceptable to appropriate images and sound one hadn't created, as long as the collage art created offered something new that differed from the original sources, something that transformed and recontextualized them. Another existing rule or principle I accepted was that it was preferable to use low art, disposable, mass produced sources and elevate them rather than to use high art sources. There was a general sense that the latter were much less malleable and inhibiting to work with being already accomplished works of art. Likewise, any source material that was extremely popular and to which audiences already had deep connections was wise to avoid. Over the decades these views have stayed largely intact but have expanded to be more open-minded to the validity of exceptions.

Originality I found to be an extremely paradoxical issue once I seriously began contemplating it. I noticed how often what was credited as innovations were imports from other fields or other nonwestern traditions. I noticed how much is invented building off of other artists' works. Maybe that's why working in genre has such a strong attraction to me since genre included precedent as a positive given. Also, I enjoy feeling part of an ongoing continuum.

Collage in particular struck me as having a very narrow and limited bandwidth of originality. I began to think of myself as "collaborating" with the creators of my source material, building upon and honoring what the creators of my source materials had done. Of course, since I wasn't getting permission to collaborate I am very much aware this is also a deeply paradoxical and illusory justification. The darker notion arose that it could be considered I was "stealing" my source materials. Because of this aspect of collage reality, making crime films has held a special interest for me, and when I make one, I mean for it to allude to and address this reality of appropriation as theft.

As for copyright, it was clearly best to avoid it entirely. It's an economic system that requires a great deal of capital to participate in. Money, that even when I was winning grants regularly and working a bit in advertising and music video, I didn't have. There was a tradition of using copyrighted pop songs and classical music in famous experimental films where clearly no permission had been granted or acquired.

My impression was that experimental film and the art world were an alternative, parallel universe that had its own separate rules. Of course, over the years potential copyright violation has kept my work from receiving certain attention and monetary recompense including being able to be screened on television and from being distributed for sale on DVD. The four cardinal rules as I understand them for artists who function outside copyright are: don't be publicly successful enough to draw the attention of the copyright holder; don't make enough money for the copyright holder to decide it's worthwhile to pursue litigation against you;

don't offend the copyright holder to the point where they're motivated to legally pursue you; don't use source material by creators who are known to be especially observant and litigious about copyright infringement—(the band U2 for instance). I've never been contacted by anyone about copyright infringement so luckily I don't seem to have violated any of these rules.

So what about with music? You have used Sinatra, Julie London, and some music that might very well have deep connections for people

Over time I was willing to risk it. But I had to believe very strongly in the film I was making and the necessity of using such a popular source material. I made the decision that these extremely popular songs were at times what I wanted and needed to work with. This desire overrode any concerns I had about the rules of what to avoid. Those rules had started to sound to me too much like the rules of the Christian afterlife—follow the rules, don't sin and go to heaven—in this case "art heaven." I stopped caring about going to "art heaven" and instead used the source materials, especially musically that I was most interested and excited about using.

The Velvet Underground is probably the riskiest choice I've ever made in terms of people having deep associations with source music I've used. But in the structure of the *Nimbus Trilogy* (2010–2011), I found a structural way to use those connections to my advantage. I created two films that used the same visual sequence but had different soundtracks—the first being Velvet's "Pale Blue Eyes," which my accompanying imagery is and isn't illustrative of the story the song's lyrics tell. (Here, again I'm using the lyrics like a screenplay.) The second soundtrack is a mixture of sound effects and Ravel and drastically changes the way the audience understands the story of 1960s NYC my images are telling.

How do you get away with using, for example, Frank Sinatra or Springsteen songs without permission?

Yeah, I'm rolling the dice, taking a risk. Somebody could come after me. But fortunately, no one has. I get a little worried sometimes. *Pony Glass* was described briefly in a New York Times review about the New York Film Festival and the Sinatra music was mentioned. Altair was described in a Pedro Almodovar film review because it was the opening short film. But nobody ever noticed that could cause me problems.

I did get flagged when The Film-Maker's Co-op tried to put *Downs Are Feminine* online with a paywall. They immediately got shut down because there was an official music video for the song from the band. Even though I had permission from the band, I didn't get it in writing, so I didn't have a leg to stand on legally.

False Aging

In 2007 or thereabouts, you made the switch to digital. Why did you hold off for so long?

I waited until I saw that digital could produce imagery that looked as good to me as 16mm. Until then I never liked the way video looked. There was also an economic aspect to my switch. I was underemployed. I had a son and a mortgage. Grants were no longer a reliable source of income. 16mm had gotten too expensive. It costs me $2K–$5K to make a ten minute film. And that wasn't going to do it for me in terms of output. I was too prolific to make one film a year, too bursting with ideas and a need and desire to work.

The first piece I made digitally was *Antigenic Drift* (2007), which explored the ugly aggressiveness of contemporary imagery. I knew that the aura of digital film's color palette would fit this imagery. It was an intentionally cold film that got a very chilly reception. During one screening, I heard a filmmaker friend tell someone how much they hated the digital white I was using. I considered this high praise because I was using digital white for how abrasive it was (lol). I wanted *Antigenic Drift* to be frightening because it was imagining a pandemic and how the spread of the virus occurred through plane travel. Digital is great at reproducing white because, unlike in an analog film print, it's not going to get dirty and scratched. In digital I could get this super pure, abrasive white that couldn't be decayed by projection.

But the real test as to whether I could keep shooting in digital instead of 16mm was if it could accurately reproduce the analog color, the mid-20th-century imagery, that I've spent the vast majority of my time making films with. I made *False Aging* (2008) next to test this out. I wasn't sure whether it was going to work but I was ecstatic when it did! Some people were even confused. They thought I'd made *False Aging* on film because of all the analog imagery. It was an interesting hybrid that way.

And one of the things I found out was that my use of digital gets reproduced in theatrical projection way better than my work in 16mm or S8 ever did. What's up on the screen includes way more of the subtleties and nuances that I actually see and make decisions about when I'm shooting than 16mm or S8 ever reproduced for me as a projected image. People often would remark to me about the powerful use of texture in my digital films as if they hadn't noticed that before in my work. Texture has always been important to me but because digital enhances texture it was like a new aspect of my work for many people. But the positive qualities didn't stop there. For me editorially, I have more freedom than I've ever had before. It's easy to repeat shots which is great for my natural attraction to repetition. And, like I said, economically it was a godsend. Now for that same $2000 that would allow me to create one 16mm film, I could create a whole feature-length series.

In your recent works you've moved to more modern sources for your material

Yes. I finally reached a point where the present felt as vital to address through contemporary imagery as the pastness of the present did through mid-20th-century imagery.

When I created my series *Circumstantial Pleasures* (2020), I was addressing what I consider the virulent neo-liberal aspects of capitalism head-on, specifically the global environmental crisis engulfing us. I wanted to depict the way systems of trade worked. Plastics became essential imagery—plastics that I had spent 20 years collecting—and they became a key element in linking all the films in the series. These films have no protagonists or narratives. The emphasis is on the products and especially their wrappings. It's about the way commerce moves, through a description of the textures, products, and waste created. The different plastics became the stars, the protagonists.

Are you still physically cutting and pasting material, or are you scanning now?

I don't scan. I still shoot in the same way I always have; the only change is the camera. I continue to work with my cutouts and other analog source materials, moving and performing them under the camera in three dimensions, just as I did with Super 8 and 16mm.

PROCESS

False Aging

When you're working on a film, what's the general process? I imagine it changes, but are there cases where you have an idea, a concept in mind, and then you seek materials that will feed that or vice versa? You find something in a box, and it triggers…

All that you describe are experiences I've had. It doesn't stay consistent. Sometimes films start improvisationally, sometimes with music, an image, an idea, or even a film genre I want to make my own version of. Sometimes I start making a film simply because I want to see what a film with a specific title will look like. My unconscious tends to randomly produce phrases—they just bubble up spontaneously. When I think they're interesting, I add them to a long list I keep. I started to make *False Aging* (2008) because I was intrigued by its title. I could pair the title with the three songs that comprise the film's soundtrack which I had previously sequenced on a mix tape I created in the mid-1990s. It was clear how the songs described the timeline of a person's life. The imagery was then suggested by and in dialogue with each song's lyrics.

There's always a high degree of improvisation. I need that spontaneity to effectively access the poetic, associative linking that is my preferred mode of montage. My films are most alive when I'm letting my unconscious lead. My unconscious tends to be way smarter and more inventive than my conscious mind, though the interplay between the two is essential. In other words, I'm working to discover what I want to express.

Usually, when I search for specific imagery, I can't find it, even when I know I have it! Over the decades, I've spent many frustrating hours on searches where I can't locate exactly what I'm looking for. However, in the process, I usually find something else that's an effective substitute or leads me in another equally fruitful direction. While working on my film *Pony Glass* (1997), I had a clear memory of seeing an image in one of my 1940s *Fortune* magazines—an illustration where a golf course foregrounded a group of industrial buildings. I spent hours combing through my *Fortunes* but could never find it. My "clear memory" was obviously of an image that didn't exist! Finally, to get what I needed, I collaged together a golf course and an industrial building-scape from two separate source illustrations. My memory was just an imagining of these juxtaposed images generated by my unconscious, which gave me insight into how unreliable my memory is.

Another aspect of this searching is that I've got lots of source material I don't remember I have. Most of the material I've accumulated, I need to look at to remember. But once I am looking at it, the themes, narratives, and ideas they suggest tend to be consistent and stable. For instance, 20 years after moving from New York to Los Angeles, I found a box that I packed up and sealed for the move but never opened once I arrived. It was full of magazines. As I leafed through one of them, I had the same exact reaction about why it could be valuable to me and how to use its imagery in a film as when I initially leafed through it in the store where it was purchased in the 1980s.

Pony Glass

My films sometimes start from juxtapositions of love songs or other types of music, but just as often, they start from collecting specific kinds of imagery. For instance, *Altair* (1994) started when I bought a whole bunch of *Cosmopolitan* magazines from the late 1940s. There was a whole world in those women's magazine illustrations that, at first, I was inspired to shoot as a B&W Noir. The period was right. But then I was seduced by the color of the magazines, which reminded me of Technicolor, and it became a color film. As a color film, *Altair* changed genres from Color Noir to Melodrama. The repeated Lullaby section of *The Firebird Suite* that became *Altair*'s soundtrack emerged by chance. I was listening to *The Firebird* while cutting out the magazine images. When I got to the Lullaby section—which I repeated twice on *Altair*'s soundtrack—I was so taken with it that I put my CD player on repeat and played that section for the next 90 minutes. It wouldn't wear out!

I felt this music could have served as the soundtrack to a classic 1940s psychodrama, from that early period of experimental film (a personal favorite and touchstone of mine) for the way it tells subjective, first-person poetic narratives. Likewise, the use of the color blue, for which *Altair* is beloved, became a significant element only by chance as well. I had this old star map, a friend had given me as a birthday present 16 years before when I was in college (another gift I initially didn't care for and thought I had no use for—LOL). The star map connected to Joseph Cornell, whose 1980 full museum retrospective at Museum of Modern Art (which I visited at least five times) became one of my most significant inspirations for choosing collage as my medium. By using the star map, I was paying homage to Cornell's use of not only astronomical images but also the color blue to evoke infinity. Finally, I picked the title *Altair* just by searching the star map for a name that attracted me—I had never encountered it before.

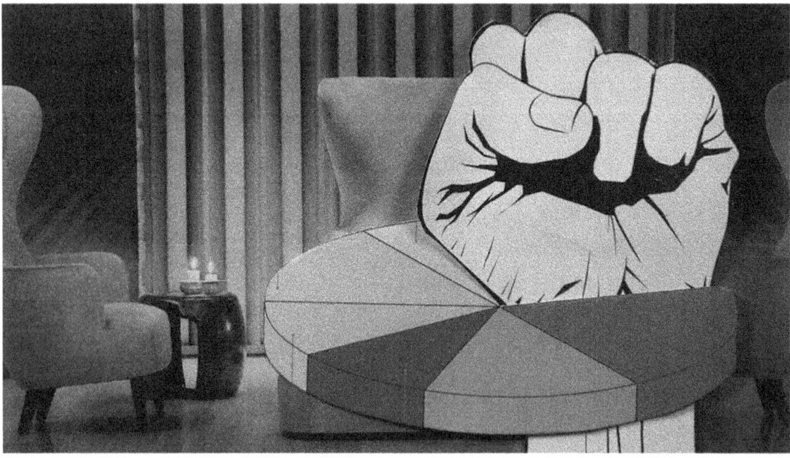

Circumstantial Pleasures

When you're selecting materials, are there times where it is just a texture, shape, or look that inspires rather than seeking materials out with an idea/theme in mind?

Yes. I grant importance to being attracted to an image via color, shape, and texture. But the themes are bound up in those qualities for me quite often.

Most of the time I'm discovering what I select to use by sifting through my image sources. There's a definite give and take between the reality of what I find and what I might be thinking I'm pursuing. The concrete reality of the images I find and choose continually modifies what I will film. Limitation figures as does chance. I'm following my intuition and my strong sense of associational connection on what to include. People often tell me they feel lost when they watch one of my films and that's probably because I'm lost on a journey of seeking and discovery while I create them. I don't really quite know where I'm going.

Let's talk a bit about editing and the approach to music. We focus on the visual collage elements but your approach to music is like making a collage as well it seems

Yes, that's true, I'm using the music as another collage element. Especially, when I'm pairing romantic pop songs to create a longer narrative. Through the continuities in the imagery, I'm trying to get you to hear the music the way I do. For instance, my film *Lethe* (2010) is set to Mahler's final symphony. Now this is quite a serious piece of music but set against the pulpy sci-fi, fantasy narrative I tell in my film, the music gets transformed into a movie soundtrack—a kind of downgrade of the Mahler symphony's gravitas.

While usually I edit my images to the music, that's not always so. For *The Pharoah's Belt*, the soundtrack was constructed after the visual edit was complete. I had to find effective entry and exit points for the Last Forever songs I was using on the film's soundtrack.

So you'll sometimes alter the visual to fit the music?

Sure, if that's what's needed, there's always a back and forth. In general, a lot of the editing is very intuitive. I don't really know how to use these digital editing programs the way they are intended to be used, so I just edit the way I edited with analog film. I put my footage on a rush line and copy what section of a shot I want to use from there.

I throw shots around timelines a lot. I'll paste in a shot that's too long and erase something I wasn't intending to replace just to see what things look like. I'm open to accidents and these chance juxtapositions. I'll place a shot on top of another and create a superimposition by lowering the opacity. If I like what I get I'll keep it. A lot of *Circumstantial Pleasures* was created with this kind of trial and error improv layering. I worked very, very quickly and instinctively. I was following impulses and discovering what was of interest to the eye instead of my mind. This sense of discovery is an important aspect of my films and why they feel alive and challenging to translate back into verbal descriptions.

What about endings? Do you have an end in mind for a film or, is it a gut feeling like it's time to jump ship?

Sometimes, things end because I'm ready to move on. Frequently, though, I like to move quickly, perfecting a film only to a certain degree. There are shots or edits that might bother me, but I decide not to fix them. I don't make perfect films or aspire to. I usually feel it's more important to move on and start fresh, to live with these little mistakes and dissatisfactions, and also to avoid overworking something until it's lifeless. Occasionally, with a film like *Daylight Moon* (2002), its essence required me to keep revising until it was as good as I could make it. It's one of my best films, and I knew it would be while I was creating it. So, part of what I'm describing is that for me—especially as someone who is prolific and fits Manny Farber's definition of a "termite"—there are different aims and levels of ambition for each individual film. Working in series also requires this: to form an effective, dynamic sequence, different films need to have different scales, aims, ambitions, and engagements.

There are also times when the ending is known to me, and it's what I'm striving to reach. Such is the case in my film *Lethe* (2009). There, I knew

Daylight Moon

where the character was going to end up—that she would realize, after crossing the river of death into the afterlife, that her life had ended. I was working to get to that dramatic climax. But *Lethe* is more explicitly narrative than most of my films.

More specifically, in terms of endings, with *Altair,* I discovered the sequencing and story I was telling on the editing table, so I didn't know what the ending would be until it emerged. I discovered how the different shots could be assembled in associative rhymes that created meanings and an oblique, suggestive narrative. I realized early on in my filmmaking that the obliqueness of my storytelling was more important than clarity. I needed to tell myself a story that I understood, even if viewers couldn't. The result was a significant structuring device for viewers, who could feel the sense of story pulling them along, remaining just out of reach, yet requiring them to fill in the blanks with their own imaginations.

MUSIC

If you're incorporating artists like Sinatra, Tobin Sprout, or Nick Drake, what generally inspires you about a particular song? Is it the lyrics? The mood?

It's a combination of all those elements. However, I need to have five or six compelling reasons to use a piece of music, something I learned from Bruce Conner and Kenneth Anger. Without sufficient reasons, the music's use can end up being superficial and merely illustrative. For instance, I used Nick Drake's "Riverman" in *Daylight Moon* for reasons of synesthesia—I perceived the music's colors as a blend of green and black.

I appreciate the map a complete song provides. It offers a structure that I didn't create but have absorbed deeply, both musically and lyrically. I aim to make you experience the music the way I do through my imagery. These pop songs become part of my work, even though I didn't compose or perform them. Pop songs often become so intertwined with people's lives that they're personalized and adapted to individual listeners' psyches. This sense of ownership is another facet of contemporary media absorption that my films address.

Lyrics have always fascinated me. They compress stories and time in a beautifully economical and efficient way. Bacharach and David even mentioned wanting their songs to tell a feature-length movie story in three minutes. Similarly, I often view the lyrics in the songs I use as screenplays. For example, in *April Snow* (2010), I used two songs with which I had a lot of listening history: the Shangri-Las' "Out in the Street" and Bruce Springsteen's "Racing in the Street." I first juxtaposed these songs on a mixtape I made back in 1986, using mixtapes as a way to sketch and test montage ideas. The Shangri-Las' song presents a teenage female perspective on a breakup, while Springsteen's song depicts a mid-20s male whose love for his car leads to his girlfriend's disillusionment. By juxtaposing these songs, I expand their thematic reach and alter their narratives. My imagery offers a different perspective than the lyrics suggest. Just as a finished feature film is not merely the script, my films interpret lyrics in a way that transforms the original stories.

When you've got a piece of music do you start just thinking about the connection with the visuals when you're listening to that song?

Yes. But I still have to go find the character and the milieu. Let's say I know it's Lois Lane, what period of Lois Lane? I have a bunch of Lois Lane comic books from different periods of the 1960s, all of which suggest different ideas about who this character is. A lot of times it's about waiting for the right juxtaposition of sound and image that provides activation.

LPS VS SINGLES

The Pettifogger

What spawned the idea to compile different short films into a feature-length series?

That comes out of a love we share, Chris: music and LPs; it's how LPs are organized. A major aesthetic experience of my life is the experience of individual songs assembling into a whole record album. So, it's not a cinematic form that I'm imitating. I mean, many filmmakers have always worked in series, but I can't say I was inspired by Hollis Frampton's work in series or Brakhage's although I admire both. The music album is the model that really set that structure for me.

When you're putting together, let's call it, "the album," how do you decide on the "singles," what fits, and the order, etc.?

There's different thematics and stylistic consistencies that define the character of each feature I create and that helps determine what can or can't be included. So, for instance in *Sixty-Six,* I was considering including *Alcestis* (2021) since it's an adaptation of the Greek myth and Euripides play and Greek myth is such an important connector throughout *66.* But I already had included *Lethe* (2010) another film that was about death and was set in the afterlife. That seemed like too much of a redundancy. Plus, I didn't want to rush my grappling with the narrative challenges *Alcestis* posed, because it was much more explicitly narrative than how I usually work and required a lot of growth on my part to successfully resolve and complete.

Sequencing is a very subtle task, trial and error is always the key. With *66 (2002–2015)*, I just had to keep viewing it. I'd watch the same sequence for several days in a row because I could only watch it once a day with fresh eyes and receive fresh insights into whether the sequence was effective. Complicating things further is the fact that I'm narcoleptic so, with a 90 minute duration, I often fell asleep which made that day's screening worthless. It was very hard, challenging work to perfect its sequence.

Then to watch a film with an audience changes it too. I toured *66* in person more than any other film I've ever made. By the end of that year there were revisions I would have made to several of the films to shorten their overall running time. The ideas for these revisions came from where I noticed the audience's attention consistently flagging. Actually, at some point I might still make these revisions.

After I premiered *The Blue Rose of Forgetfulness* at the London Film Festival in October 2022 I was dissatisfied with its sequence. Before *The Blue Rose's* U.S. premiere at the Academy Film Museum in Los Angeles in February 2023, I made what had been the last film, *Monogram* (2019), the first. *Monogram* functioned better as an introductory film than as a summary film coming at the end. I kept the rest of the sequencing intact and now *The Blue Rose of Forgetfulness* has for me the most satisfying aural sequencing build of any of my feature series.

Erigone's Daughter

Circumstantial Pleasures is the feature I had the most challenges with as a sequence, to the point where I actually had to take apart what I thought were finished films, some of which had already screened publicly, and make a revised version of them. Even in the eleventh hour, just before CP's enthusiastically received premiere at Light Industry in February of 2020, I realized the second film, *Ramification Lesions (microbial stress)* [2020] was too long, and I had to cut three minutes out of it!

It's like an ouija board or a seance and you're the medium

Right. There's that excitement of exploration and discovery all in the present tense. Language and clear understanding can be important and foregrounded but my ultimate aesthetic strength is creating a mystery, a journey.

In some cases, you use recent films, but in others, like 66 (2015), you went back as far as 2002

To clarify with *66*—2002 was just a start date for beginning to work with the imagery that became a quartet of films included in the sequence—*Ichor* (2013), *Saturn's Diary* (2014), *The Silver Age* (2015), *Orphacles* (2013)—none of which were completed before 2013. These are all of a piece since they use the same characters pulled from a comic book adaptation of the 1960s tv show Burke's Law. These comic book characters' beautiful, saturated color was my initial inspiration for working with this imagery. I chose to include these films in *66* because they are male-centric and poetically elliptical. Whereas *Helen of T* (2013), *Erigone's Daughter* (2014), *Lip Print (Venus)* (2012), and *Lethe* (2010) are female-centric and more explicitly narrative. These two "quartets" become the spine of *66* structurally.

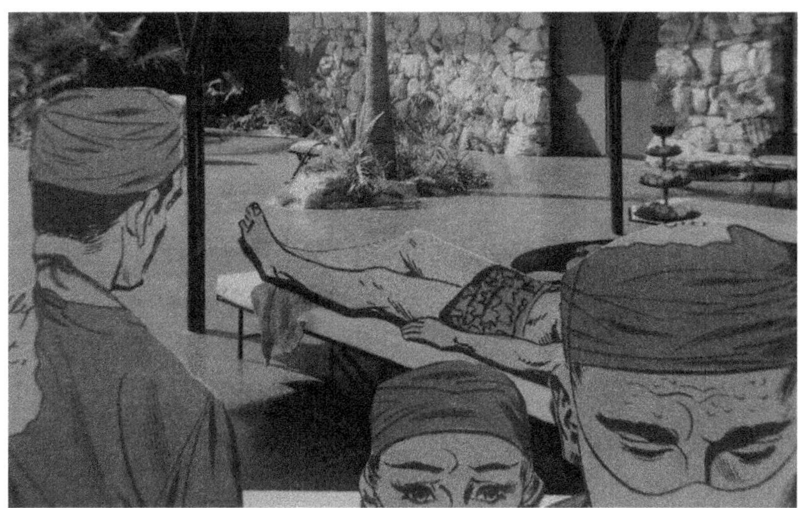

Helen of T

I had other choices about what to include in *66* that I went back and forth about—for instance *Ambrosia* (2014) and *August 19, 1966 (Jupiter sends a Message)* neither of which includes the kind of mythopoetic comic book imagery that the eight films mentioned above do. Ultimately I decided I wanted to include both these films because they described the era of the 1960s so effectively. By including them I was expanding the range of imagery of the series and linking these two films to the Greek mythological tilt of the rest of the series but only through their titling. And speaking of this titling, I chose to inconsistently use the Greek or Roman names of different gods on purpose. Often, I picked the Roman because I liked them better but also because it put on the table the idea that even in ancient times, this mythology was being appropriated, transformed, and adapted just as I was doing in the new millennium connecting it to the 1960s.

Was it tougher to work on longer individual films like The Pharoah's Belt and The Pettifogger, to stay in that world for so long?

Yeah. *The Pharaoh's Belt* is only 43 minutes, but I poured everything I had into it. I was trying to make a feature-length film of over 60 minutes but the extra duration just wasn't there for me. It was a slow process that took two years. I'd shoot 2–4 rolls of film and then I'd have to wait to get the energy, inspiration, and imagery to shoot more. It was like a mostly dry desert well where to get a bucket of water you've got to patiently wait for the water to rise out of and above the sand.

Working on *The Pharaoh's Belt* for two years, I realized midway through that I needed a vacation. Especially from thinking about childhood. So I took some time off and created both *Altair* and *Downs Are Feminine* and at least made it into adolescence!

THINKING ABOUT NARRATIVE

You've spoken in the past about your work short circuiting language. Could you elaborate on that a bit?

My associational approach to montage is addressing the audience's unconscious to the same or a greater degree than it addresses their conscious minds. People often report to me that they find themselves thinking about my films several weeks after they see them. There's this gradual capsule release effect my films seem to have that I think is related to the difficulty of describing them in words. Frequently I like to play a complete song because it gives the audience a linear map they can hold onto while I visually digress into poetic and associative montages. Ultimately the visuals become dominant and create a revery for the audience that is similar to the state I shoot and edit my films in. Linearity gradually gets left behind. Seeing one of my films in isolation often gives people the impression that they're easy to talk about or describe. After all, they have a lot of pop touch points. But seeing a series of them tends to overwhelm this sense of clarity.

For example, near the end of my recent film *Alcestis*, the title character walks through an endless Chinese restaurant—a loop of the same background postcard passing by over and over again. Alcestis looks caught in the circularity of this space and time. A friend of mine said he had a strong emotional reaction to this sequence but didn't know why and couldn't organize his feelings into words. I was very happy to hear this as it is a climactic moment but a subtle one. Alcestis is beginning to transition back to the living world even before Hercules arrives to rescue her home from the underworld. What's felt is as important in my films as what's clearly understood.

Watching your films is often like trying to recount a dream and convey it to somebody

Yeah, if you could show them the images. If you could show them the dream, they might understand more of it.

But you're showing us the dream in a way, but then when we try to put it into language, it doesn't go easily

Yes, as the viewer you are awake and you would think that would make it easier to describe and recount but how I'm sequencing images and conveying the exposition, even in my most clearly narrative pieces like Alcestis, doesn't allow for that. In fact, I often can't remember how I've sequenced things either. For this reason, when I do screenings with a Q&A, I almost always watch the films with the audience so at least they're fresh in my mind lol.

You've often used the phrase "the pastness of the present" to describe some of your work. What exactly do you mean by that?

I would say it describes almost all of my work. It's a historical perspective through which I view the world. How long ago was something created? We are surrounded by all kinds of artifacts—movies, music, furniture, cars—created in different eras. They are all very much in the present tense but also bring their histories with them, just like collage images do. We often ignore and take their creation dates for granted. With my films, I'm most often using imagery from mid-20th-century America. But I keep finding that my point of view of and relationship to these images shifts as the present changes and filters them. As I got deeper into this idea I started to wonder when exactly does something become old? When does it stop being considered new and part of the past?

With the more autobiographical films, how would you describe those? You are making a film about the past but from the present perspective. It's a child's perspective but created by an adult in the present.

I often make things as a grownup through the filter of a child; my memory of being a child. I'm trying to access that sense of wonder that's in childhood and its freshness and newness of discovery. Childhood's sense of play. But it's by using all these images and sounds that are mostly outmoded. It's paradoxical how it all spins on itself.

I was just thinking about how our memories are often clouded by false images. Sometimes what we think is our memory might actually be a fragment from a movie or a broadcast. For example, I'm convinced I saw the Stanley Cup-winning goal in 1971 during a game between the Montreal Canadiens and the Chicago Black Hawks, but it might have been years later in a replay.

Yeah, I know what you mean. I've had many similar experiences where media and memory get intertwined. It's common for media, whether it's snapshots or home movies, to replace one's own memories. I stay on the lookout for these kinds of distortions and find them very useful for my collaging. For instance, the title for my film *Yesterday's Glue* (1990) came about because of a cheap boombox I had in my East Village apartment. I was listening to an old Marianne Faithfull song, *Yesterday's Blue*, but on my lo-fi system's poor speakers, it distinctly sounded like she was singing "Yesterday's Glue." I thought, wow, what a great title! But then something even stranger happened. One day, a friend asked me if I got the title for *Yesterday's Glue* from Marianne Faithfull's *Yesterday's Blue*. She clearly had a similarly shitty stereo!

Saturn's Diary

This is similar to how I came up with the title for this book. I was listening to the Lana Del Rey song "Honeymoon," which you used in your film Capitulations Promise. I was convinced she was singing "dreaming a way of life," but it's actually "dreaming away your life."

I love how you switched it! There's a fascinating amount of signal-to-noise distortion in media transmission. Our brains often mishear or distort what we absorb to better fit our personal or subjective experiences. This adaptation and personalization of media sources is one of the main subjects of my work.

Not long ago, I found some home movies from my childhood. When I watch them, there's a sense of safety and comfort but also an underlying emptiness. I smile and feel love and family, yet there's a touch of grief. These moments are gone, as are most of the people in the films. I see a version of myself, but it's not me—I don't remember that particular experience. I often feel this way with your films. You take all these materials and create your own playground, yet it's not real.

Hmm... You've described a number of complex personal and subjective experiences. While my work often firmly locates itself in the imaginary, that doesn't make it any less real. Nor do I see how the sense of lived time my films induce is any less real. On a descriptive level, these types of media experiences are defining characteristics of contemporary life in highly saturated urban societies. I also believe there's much more interpenetration between documentary and fiction than most people like to acknowledge.

I don't agree that I only create my own playground. Yes, my personal relationship to the source materials is palpable, but I also leave many images with trace elements that reassert or remind viewers of their original context.

This duality creates a frictive juxtaposition that punctures and deflates whatever new fiction I'm creating. My films oscillate between first-person and third-person perspectives.

You've talked about being a "re-animator." There must be a certain satisfaction or sense of power in that. It's like being a kid, playing God with all these toys. I could make Star Wars figures do whatever I wanted. I had hockey cards and made up imaginary games where I could ensure my team won and my players scored.

Huh… I played differently than you. My older brother taught me a basketball game using toy soldiers as players. When I played, I never felt in control—the games would unfold on their own. That was a huge part of the pleasure for me: the ability to let go and be so immersed that I didn't have control. It felt like the game was happening like a real basketball game I was watching on TV. I inhabited all the different players. I suppose that's a form of god-like omnipresence, but if I tried to make one team win, it would have felt like cheating and disrupted my immersion and pleasure. To a large extent, this is how I feel when making my films—they unfold as they flow through me, and I get to inhabit their worlds. Yes, I'm creating them, but I'm both in control and not in control. They're highly spontaneous and improvisational, with all the surprises that entails.

But now that you've got me thinking, there were moments during childhood play when I did exercise excessive control. I have an early memory from when I was four or five. My first best friend and I would play with toy soldiers, and I'd dictate the lines of dialogue. I'd say, "Now you say this," and then he would repeat it, and I'd continue with my next line. I was directing and writing the script.

Orson Welles of the playground!

Hahahaha.

In one interview you mentioned the need to initially engage the viewer before delivering a shock or jolt that takes them in an unexpected direction. Can you expand on that and provide an example?

Yes, I recognized that Surrealism by the time I inherited it was too familiar as a genre; shock or surprise was very challenging to create. But I realized if I could get viewers used to me working in one engagement that they expected to continue I could make a radical change in engagement that would create the kind of surprise and shock the Surrealists were after. In my first cutout film created for my series *Tales of the Forgotten Future: For the Rest of Your Natural Life*, the early imagery is super flat cutouts. Gradually this flatness is interrupted by various cutouts mounted and puppet-ed on sticks that enter and hover above the cutouts lying flat on the picture plane. But the climactic action occurs when a 3-D plastic fly swatter descends through the frame to crush a paper fly.

I remain excited about these kinds of disruptive changes in engagement. A good recent example of this occurs in the sequencing of *Blue Sun* (2020) the fourth film of my feature-length series *The Blue Rose of Forgetfulness (2022). Blue Sun* follows two films that use torch songs by female singers for their soundtracks—*Swollen Kisses* and *Capitulations Promise*—and follows their aural lushness with the equally lush backward Sibelius (a continuity that helps maintain the flow), which, ultimately, gives way to the matter of fact, pragmatism of a street soundscape of bird chirps and passing cars in the film's final third. This soundscape is set against the visuals of B&W secret agent comic book drawings I shot on a light box to illuminate both sides of the comic book page to capture the interesting, created by chance superimpositions. The film looks like it should be narrative because there's so much overtonal narrative information exploding from the secret agent story, but if you're trying to find a narrative you won't, it's not there. Instead, *Blue Sun* deeply addresses your eye, which is a huge shift of engagement from the preceding two films, which offer clearer visuals with accessible narrative opacities and emotional arcs. This shift is a kind of rupture and, of course, a lot to ask from my audience. I've been very gratified by how many positive comments I've received from audience members that *Blue Sun* is their favorite film of the series. What that tells me is that I nailed the sequencing.

CATHARSIS, PRODUCTIVITY, AND FUNDING

Lewis Klahr in Studio

That leads me to another topic I had written down, which is about catharsis

Catharsis? I believed in it and wanted it to have an impact on my films when I was young. I thought, "I'll make this film about my childhood and then be done with this old mid-20th-century imagery and work with contemporary appropriated images on adult themes." But that's not what happened. The film I made, instead of being a definitive and final statement, merely bent my fascination with mid-20th-century imagery in a new direction. Something my mentor, the eminent film scholar Tom Gunning, alerted me to is that there's tremendous freedom of expression and adaptability in the outmoded.

You've been quite prolific. How often are you working on something?

Almost always. I'm prolific because I have a lot of impulses about what to do—my brain generates ideas quickly. I've always discovered what I'm expressing through creation rather than just thinking or writing, so I needed an art practice that allowed me to work daily. My approach to cutout animation is also straightforward: I shoot tableaus that use a lot of stillness and small movements, which makes my images easy and quick to shoot. That might sound like a compromise, but it isn't—stillness, minimal movement, and tableaus are deeply interesting to me as rigorous aesthetic choices. This stillness characterized the mainstream animations I watched as a child—Speed Racer, Gigantor, and the early Marvel television cartoons.

Limited animation

Yes. They had to produce content quickly, and I engaged with those cartoons as expressions of the beauty of limited means. While there's an art to this approach that is every bit as demanding as a maximalist one, it also makes it much quicker to shoot things. When I'm on a roll, I can shoot two or three minutes in a single day, and I've always been a fast editor.

But there's another, deeper reason for my prolific output: I wanted to live a thousand different lives. Making films was the only way I knew to approximate that. I needed to push through to the next film as quickly as possible because there was always a new world I wanted to enter, a new life I wanted to experience. Now, in my late 60s, that drive is still present but is shaped more by questions like: What haven't I done or done enough of? What do I want to revisit?

Given how prolific you are, projects must overlap.

For most of my creative life, I typically worked on one film at a time, immersing myself completely until it was finished. But when I turned 60 and had just completed *66*, I made a rather impulsive decision. I thought, "I'm at some kind of expressive peak. I'm going to start several new projects and explore what it's like to work on many films simultaneously." As a result, I ended up with about 15 films in progress and am still working through that backlog. I had hoped that *The Blue Rose of Forgetfulness* (2021) would help me finish that cycle, but it seems that working on multiple projects at once has become my new norm. It might also stem from a sense of urgency, given that I'm unsure how much more time I'll have to be creatively effective.

Right now I'm working on two new feature-length series that are nearing completion and part of an umbrella series I've titled *From 45 to 33*. It'll have different parts like my Super 8 series *Tales of the Forgotten Future* did.

Has your speed changed over the years? I know some artists who were quite prolific early on but then became maybe a bit more particular over time

Probably slower because I'm more demanding. It's a bit harder for me to work. I've always questioned what's worth doing but now that's even more pronounced. But I haven't slowed that much—I'm still prolific. And there's films I've brainstormed and collected materials for that I can't wait to give my full attention.

You need to be teaching or have another job. You can't make a living off what you're doing

There was a brief period in the late 1980s and early 1990s when I was able to live off a combination of grants, rentals, and commercial work. I think one year I made 75 grand. That was the peak of it, not very much money but enough to grant me my freedom to work full-time as an artist for the next couple of years.

Do you still go after any funding at all?

There's not a lot of opportunities in the U.S. The last things I received were a grant from Creative Capital when they were a new organization around the year 2000 [non-profit funding group] and one out here in Los Angeles around 2008, that's a city grant for mid-career artists. There's just not a lot of funding out here in California for what I do. Back in NYC when I was young and formative I always did well with grants because my stuff didn't look like anyone else's and would stand out. Also, it had an accessibility factor and that "hit single" thing we talked about. I had a nice run where I steadily got grants from the late 1980s–1990s. But that was also a time of peak public funding for the arts in the U.S. I've also made some money in the gallery world from sales but never enough to live on.

I have to teach to make ends meet.

Are there films you'd rather forget, that maybe didn't work out the way you'd hoped?

Many. But I think they're a necessary part of my continuum and if I didn't fail, I wouldn't have been able to create my most appreciated and successful films. For instance, in the mid-1990s I made two scripted, cutout story films that were complete and utter failures! It's no coincidence that afterward, having learned from my mistakes, I made one of my most revered films—my poetic narrative *Pony Glass*.

If you were to choose a few films that you are most proud of, what would they be and what makes them resonate with you so strongly?

I hate to pick because different films have different objectives and I like my body of work as a whole including its failures more than I like any one film. But to honor your question *Daylight Moon* and *False Aging* are the two that get closer than anything else to capturing what I've always been after to describe about lived time.

Lewis Klahr at Work

2

Ghosts of a Different Dream: *The Collision of Memory and Mass Media*[1]

> But certainly for the present age, which prefers the sign to the thing signified, the copy to the original, representation to reality, the appearance to the essence...[2]

Many are familiar with Plato's allegory of the cave. In this story, people are chained inside a cave, facing a wall, with a fire behind them. Shadows of objects carried along a road behind the fire are cast onto the cave wall. These cave dwellers only see the shadows—mere reflections and half-truths—believing them to be reality. They are unaware that they're seeing only copies of copies.

Plato couldn't have predicted how prescient this allegory would become in the modern world, where we are inundated with images—photographs, films, television, the internet—every second of every day. In such a world of mechanical reproduction, distinguishing truth from fiction has become more difficult than ever.

A few years ago, I had my grandparents' 8mm home movies from the late 1960s and early 1970s digitized. In many of the frames, I appear as a toddler. In one film, I'm at a picnic table, trying to drink from an empty beer bottle (I'd master filled ones later). Until I watched this footage, I had no memory

DOI: 10.1201/9781003427223-2

of these events. Now, after seeing the images, they've seeped into my mind. I may one day believe I genuinely remember that picnic. The footage shows a very young version of me while family members play badminton in the background. But, other than that, I have no real sense of the context.

So, is there anything wrong with that?

Well, yes and no.

On the one hand, it's nice to access forgotten experiences. Sometimes they trigger deeper reflections about the time, the people, and the setting. But the images are just traces—misleading cut-outs of an experience I can never truly access. As Susan Sontag pointed out, the problem isn't just that we remember through images; it's that we often end up only remembering the images themselves. They can override more meaningful forms of understanding or remembering.[3]

We tend to assume photos and videos are truthful representations. Rarely do we stop to consider that an image is framed by someone who made deliberate choices about what to include and exclude. We do this less with paintings or written accounts. When we learn an image or video was staged or faked, we feel embarrassed for having been deceived because we instinctively trusted the image. In the age of deepfakes and AI-generated imagery, we need to rethink this uncritical trust we place in images.

Images also shift our focus from the present to the past. We live in an era of nostalgia. Rehashed storylines, remakes, and social media are cluttered with echoes of the past, often curated as if they were fully lived moments. The images give us a false sense of familiarity with these past events. We scroll through our photo galleries, feeling as though we've captured everything, yet, in doing so, we may have missed the real moments.

In the early 1990s, Lewis Klahr filmed his best friend Mark Lapore's wedding on 16mm. Years later, he asked Lapore, a fellow filmmaker, if he had ever looked at the footage. Lapore replied, "No, I don't want to lose my memories of the experience."[4] He feared that the filmed images would displace the reality in his mind.

Sontag, writing in *On Photography* (1977), couldn't have imagined how much more complicated our relationship with images would become with the advent of digital technology, the internet, and social media. Today, we aren't just surrounded by family photos or home videos; we're constantly bombarded with commercial, political, and pop culture imagery.

But how do these external images influence us? Have they infiltrated not just our memories but also our desires and goals? How many of us have had our ideas of love, romance, or success shaped by Hollywood, or by advertising that persuades us to buy diamond rings or follow particular rituals? As

Guy Debord argued in *The Society of the Spectacle* (1967), society has shifted from being to having, and from having to appearing. Until the post-World War II era, people primarily existed by being, by participating in reality. But with the rise of consumerism, owning things became more important than simply being. Today, the emphasis is on appearance—on how we present ourselves to the world.

We no longer look at the world; we look at screens. On these screens, we see stories about distant places and people, stories that often don't impact us directly. We become passive observers, distanced from the reality of the world, our communities, and even ourselves. Debord called this "the spectacle"—a collection of commodifiable images that distract and alienate us.

We are living in an updated version of Plato's cave, trapped in a house of mirrors that confuse and distract us. Those mirrors are the films, TV shows, social media, and video games that dominate our attention. Even when we want to enact change, meaningful conversations are difficult to have because we're constantly fed representations of representations, never the reality.

Our personal mythologies, curated on social media, are another layer of the spectacle. We carefully select images and stories to craft how we want others to perceive us. Our social media profiles become exhibitions, where we are both the subject and curator, presenting a polished, simplified version of ourselves. But these mythologies lack substance. They are commodified spectacles in which we become brands, presenting the appearance of a life far more complex than the narrative we curate online.

Lewis Klahr's work, which frequently employs mid-20th-century consumer and pop culture imagery to explore personal and collective memory, operates at the intersection of nostalgia, consumerism, and mass media. His films often examine how public and private images intersect with, and sometimes hijack, our memories. In several of his works, Klahr merges autobiography and fiction, using appropriated consumer imagery, home movies, and found photographs to create what he terms "media autobiography." He reflects, "I became interested in memory and history, and how those two intersect: their inaccuracies, the forgetting involved in remembering."[5]

In his autobiographical series *Pictures Books for Adults* (1983–1985), Klahr delves into various aspects of his 1960s childhood.

Pulls (1985) juxtaposes home movies with footage from cartoons and war films—genres young Klahr enjoyed. Though a relatively simple film, it illustrates an internal conflict between personal memories and pop culture imagery, as though a young mind struggles to reconcile the realities of family life with the distractions of media. The film portrays a child processing the complexities of family, the fear of war (Vietnam, Cold War), and the alluring escapism of cartoons.

In *Candee's 16!* (1984), Klahr opens with images of a 45 rpm single, "Countdown Sixteen" by Candee Weinstein, once owned by his sister. This recording's audio is paired with home movie footage, sci-fi films, Godzilla movies, and scenes from the 1960s *Spider-Man* series. The mashup becomes a meditation on coming of age, with Spider-Man's Peter Parker reflecting on his transformation—paralleling Klahr's own near-fatal car accidents. Klahr reinterprets found footage into a generational narrative, highlighting the dark transition from youth to adulthood, and perhaps the lives cut short by the Vietnam War.

In *1966* (1984), Klahr structures a narrative of a year in a ten-year-old's life through the lens of a vintage calendar. The film fuses comic book images, children's book illustrations, and home movies, creating a nostalgic yet melancholic portrait of childhood. The delicate sound of a music box captures the passage of time and the fragments of memory lost to it.

Klahr's *The Pharaoh's Belt* (1994) culminates his exploration of childhood. Using consumer and pop culture images as gateways to his past, the film suggests that these very images sometimes obstruct memory. Klahr highlights the hollowness of consumer culture, as a blindfolded child searches for meaning amid a house constructed from consumer materials. This echoes Guy Debord's critique of modern life as "an immense accumulation of spectacles" where lived experience is reduced to representations.[6]

Film historian Tom Gunning notes in his analysis of *The Pharoah's Belt*, "the products of industrial capitalism, those produced within the cycles of

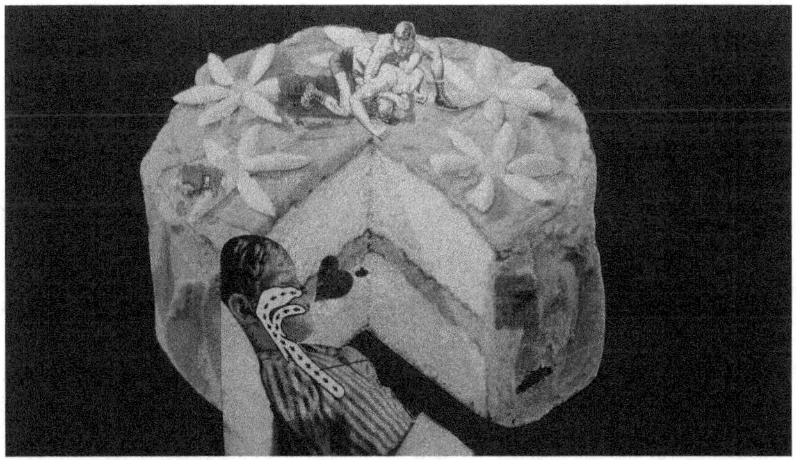

The Pharoah's Belt

fashion, attempt to re-enchant the world, hiding the inhuman face of capitalism with the mask of myth, nature or fate, enthralling consumers by stimulating a desire they can never fulfill."[7]

Gunning argues that consumer culture thrives by creating an endless cycle of disappointment and renewed hope, where each new product promises fulfillment but ultimately fails, forcing consumers into perpetual dissatisfaction.

Klahr's films, however, resist this capitalist imperative to forget. Instead, he appropriates these consumer fragments to uncover personal and collective memories long obscured by commercial culture. His use of smiling, wide-eyed figures from advertisements, initially evoking hope, transforms into something eerie, their forced joy revealing the emptiness of the consumer-driven narrative.

I understand the contradiction in Klahr's approach—using images to unearth dormant memories, much like I did when watching my grandmother's home movies. This is why I refer to this process as a complex intersection. While mass media imagery can often hijack our personal experiences, Klahr demonstrates how we can reclaim and repurpose those same images for our own narratives. Throughout his childhood films, it's as though Klahr is attempting to cut through the haze of capitalist and consumerist clutter to rediscover his true self, his family, and the reality of what once was. In doing so, he seeks not only to make sense of the past but also to better understand how it shapes the present, which was birthed from that same convoluted history.

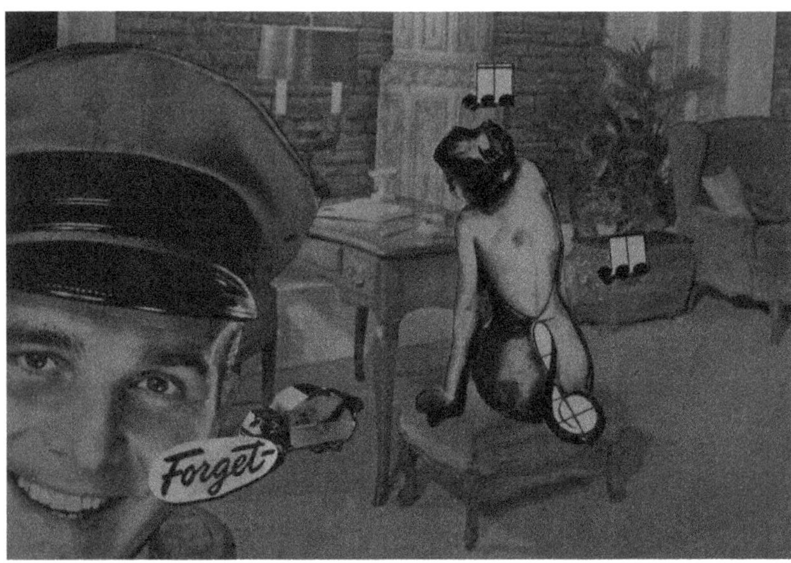

The Pharoah's Belt

> Images are indeed able to usurp reality because first of all a photograph is not only an image, an interpretation of the real; it is also a trace, something directly stenciled off the real, like a footprint or a death mask.[8]

Images are never presented to us in an unbiased manner. They are always crafted to elicit a particular emotional response, with the creator deciding what to include and exclude. Even on a personal level, when we send a headshot—whether for a film festival or online dating—we carefully choose that image to project a specific impression. Yet, there's only so much we can control.

While Klahr's films primarily explore childhood through mass media imagery, he also made several films using photographs that raise questions about the potency and legitimacy of images, and how easily we can subvert or alter their original intent. In these films, Klahr "heists" other people's personal photographs and transforms them into his own imaginings. The private turns public, as we become voyeurs of someone else's altered reality.

Photographs, as Sontag suggested, can fabricate "a new parallel reality that makes the past immediate while underscoring its comic and tragic ineffectuality." They transform the present into the past, and the past into something distant. Photos also alter the self. Seeing a photo of ourselves can feel unreal, as though we're seeing a side of ourselves for the first time. In a sense, a photograph objectifies that moment, freezing it in time, and removing it from our control. Anyone with access to the image can manipulate it.

Part 4 of Klahr's series *Tales of the Forgotten Future* (1988–1991) features a trio of films that deal with found photographs, raising questions about authenticity, history, memory, and time.

In *Station Drama* (1990),[9] Klahr blends found black-and-white photographs with original images of a female protagonist. The jittery, scratchy feel creates an illusion of authenticity, as though we're watching old newsreel footage. However, Klahr photographed an actress in various poses and inserted her into the found footage. The result is an Amelia Earhart-inspired story of a female pilot who achieves success but falls prey to the machinations of powerful men. The past is invaded by the present (through Klahr's manipulation) to reveal hidden truths of the past—racism, sexism, and colonialism.

"A lot of the older appropriated imagery in *Station Drama* is taken from a 1930s encyclopedia, *The Wonderland of Knowledge*," Klahr explains. The film originally began as live action, but Klahr abandoned it.

> Using photos of an actor gave me more control, especially in terms of character consistency. It was also fun to work with actors and costume them. It is also related to comic books—there's a European style of comics called *Foto Roman* that uses actors as comic book imagery, which Fellini's *The White Sheik* depicts.[10]

The Life of Naomi Lang

Untitled (The Life of Naomi Lang) (1991) uses eight photo albums from a woman's life, which Klahr found in a California bookstore. It's poignant that such personal, once-important photos ended up in the dustbin of history. Klahr reconstructs Lang's life through these photos, organizing them chronologically, with one flashback to earlier images. The film covers Lang's life from birth to death, blending presence and absence. While the photos capture real moments from Lang's life, they are incomplete. Everything outside the frame is lost, leaving us with fragments.

The audience may believe they're watching a true document of a woman's life, but it's all imagined, showing how easily images can be manipulated. Still, Klahr's treatment of Lang is touching and respectful, never mocking. There's a sense of loneliness in Lang's life—no romantic partner or children are shown, only her loyalty to her dog. The fact that these personal photos were abandoned adds a layer of tragedy.

Ultimately, these images are unsatisfactory fragments without context, incomplete pieces of a puzzle. Each photo is part of a life that was lived but can never be fully understood through the images alone. When we see Lang's life through these photos, it feels collected, not experienced. The photos attempt to simplify and control existence, rather than just *being*. In the end, they don't tell us anything substantial about Naomi Lang—they are mere fragments of a life, much like consumer images meant to be consumed, blurring the line between personal photos and commercial imagery.

The Life of Naomi Lang

Actuality

Actuality (1991) takes less personal photos, using those found in the 10-volume *Burton Holmes Lectures* (1901). Holmes, a pioneer of travelogue films, provided a window into exotic lands for American audiences, creating a kind of "armchair travel" experience. Klahr uses these photos to recreate the feel of early actuality films, cutting out images of people and placing them in different backgrounds. The result is a tribute to early documentary films that also questions the authenticity of the original images. Though the film's cut-out figures may appear comical, Klahr's faux-documentary is no more fictional than the originals, which likely staged and erased important social and political issues.

In *The Aperture of Ghostings* trilogy—comprising *Elsa Kirk* (1999), *Catherine Street* (2001), and *Creased Robe Smile*(2001)—Klahr uses three different contact sheets of women found in a New York thrift store. Unlike his work with Naomi Lang, Klahr constructs fictional narratives around these women. The photos of Elsa Kirk are especially poignant, suggesting she may have aspired to be an actress. (Through conversations with her family and friends, Klahr discovered that Kirk had a career as a working model in New York City.) For her story, Klahr imagines a crime narrative, allowing Kirk to star in a mythologized version of her own life.

In *Catherine Street*, Klahr combines a contact sheet of an Asian woman with found materials to create a fictional tale about her life as an immigrant worker in the U.S. *Creased Robe Smile* features a woman photographed in playful poses, bordering on camp. Though Klahr initially found her plain, he eventually became intrigued by her upside-down photos, discovering a hidden beauty.

In *Creased Robe Smile*, Klahr places the "found" woman into an imagined musical melodrama (highlighted by the song "Somewhere" from *West Side Story*) about a pregnant couple who struggle to be together. The contact sheet shows a playful yet plain-looking woman photographed upside down on a bed, giving her a starlet wannabe vibe. Her poses, in general, are so forced and star-craving that they border on camp, resembling social media selfies or dating site profile pictures.

Elsa Kirk

Creased Robe Smile was the most challenging of the three for Klahr:

> I wasn't attracted to the woman and thought her to be very plain, despite the fact that she's the only one of the three in a state of undress. However, the intimacy of the photos cued me into what I wanted to depict. Ultimately, I ended up caring about this woman the most out of the three—and discovered that the photographer was onto something by shooting her upside down—that she was very beautiful upside down.

Klahr's 2012 film *Album* uses images from his own family archive. Side one shows bar mitzvah photos from 1962 and 1969, while side two features found photos of a Black soldier. The juxtaposition of the polished bar mitzvahs with the loose, fragmented soldier's story adds complexity. The audio tracks accompanying the images—a book about Quicksilver Messenger Service and another about Tom Verlaine—further highlight the cultural clash between the conservative, polished bar mitzvah scenes and the raw, unpredictable world of rock and roll.

The soldier's story is particularly intriguing, with photos of him in training and with friends. References to a child and an estranged mother hint at a personal history marked by heartbreak or loss. The ripped photos suggest a fractured relationship, adding layers of mystery and tragedy.

Album reflects the limitations and power of photographs. Klahr takes these fragments of lives and turns them into meditations on class, race, and culture. His work with personal materials contrasts with his use of mass media images. "I treat personal found materials more as documents, meant

Album – Bar Mitzvah 1962

Album – Bar Mitzvah 1969

for the audience to notice for their reportorial aspect," Klahr explains. "This aspect doesn't get erased, even when I build fiction around them."[11]

Images are a gateway to the past, attempts to contact another reality. But what we gain from these images is often sentimental and limited—knowledge at a bargain price. When we see *Naomi Lang*, *Elsa Kirk*, or *Album*, we glimpse fragments of lives we can never fully understand. These people no longer exist; only their photos remain.

NOTES

1 I'm indebted to Stephen West's marvelously passionate, lucid, and accessible podcast, *Philozophize This!*, especially the episodes on Sontag, Debord and Roland Barthes.
2 Ludwig Feuerbach, *The Essence of Christianity*. New York: Calvin Blanchard, 1885, p. 10.
3 Susan Sontag, *Regarding the Pain of Others*. New York: Picador, 2003, p. 89.
4 Interview with the author, January/February 2023.
5 Interview with the author, February 2023.
6 Guy Debord, *The Society of the Spectacle*. Paris: Critical Editions, 2021, p. 1.
7 Tom Gunning, *Lewis Klahr's the Pharoah's Belt and the Amnesia of Memory*, a paper for the Conference *Der Blick der Moderne*, Vienna, June, 1996.
8 Susan Sontag, *On Photography*. London: Penguin Books, 2019, p. 165.
9 *Station Drama* was inspired by pioneering aviatrix Beryl Markham's autobiography/memoir *West with the Night*.
10 Email exchange with the author, February 2024.
11 Interview with the author, October 2023.

Styles We Paid For

3

> Myth hides nothing and flaunts nothing: It distorts; myth is neither a lie nor a confession. It is an inflexion.[1]

We often consider ourselves free-thinking, independent beings born into a world where anything is available to us, as if life were a drive-thru buffet. But is that truly the case? Are our experiences random, or are they shaped by the social, political, economic, and cultural realities of our time? Our expressions, gestures, and habits are also tightly woven into this complex system—so subtly that we often fail to realize the system's profound impact on us.

In the 1970s, when I was a kid, my heroes were athletes, rock stars, and comic book characters. These figures seemed perfect—living lives we could only dream of. I consumed every media story about Pete Townshend or my favorite hockey players. But the problem was that the media presented

The Silver Age

DOI: 10.1201/9781003427223-3

only a limited, distorted view of these individuals. I saw what they did on stage or the ice—their artistic performances. If glimpses of their private lives appeared, they were homogenized and manufactured. We weren't told about their affairs, addictions, or misbehavior. Instead, we were fed mythologies designed to encourage us to worship, adore, and consume.

There are other myths too—specifically, Greek myths. I didn't encounter these until much later in life. Unlike modern myths, Greek mythology-inspired contemplation rather than blind adulation. Today, our society adores celebrities in much the same way people once revered gods. As Karen Armstrong writes in *A Short History of Myth*, "Elvis Presley and Princess Diana were both made into instant mythical beings, even objects of religious cult. But there is something unbalanced about this adulation."[2] The original purpose of myth was not mere admiration but guidance—stories to help us live meaningful lives. However, modern society consumes myths passively, focusing more on idolization than transformation.

Myths were originally stories we created, "to place our lives in a larger setting, that revealed an underlying pattern, and gave us a sense that, against all the depressing and chaotic evidence to the contrary, life had meaning and value."[3]

Myths were once narratives that guided us in the face of life's uncertainties. These tales gave life structure, revealing that we were part of a universal essence. They were never intended to be factual but were fictional constructs designed to help us face mortality with acceptance.

In the modern world, however, this relationship with myth has changed. Robert Graves' *Greek Myths* have been replaced by the mass media, which delivers new myths daily. As Stephen West puts it, "What mythology does so well is turn history into nature."[4] Our cultural constructions—like ideas about what it means to be American—are presented as though they are fixed truths, unchangeable parts of nature.

Today's myths encourage passivity, prompting us to worship, consume, and accept. This is where the danger lies: we accept the illusion of myths as truth, saying things like, "That's just how it is," or, "It is what it is." Roland Barthes, in his landmark book *Mythologies*, argues that modern myths have evolved into ideologies that support the interests of those in power.

Barthes explains how media myths carry hidden political and economic messages that shape our worldview. Fox News, podcasts, advertisements, books, movies, and YouTube all contribute to these modern myths. Barthes believed that to truly understand the world, we must deconstruct these myths, uncovering how they shape our assumptions and limit our perspective. Barthes argued that myths "immobilize the world" and present themselves as universal truths, confining us within their constraints. He described myths as "nothing but this ceaseless, untiring solicitation, this insidious and inflexible demand that all men recognize themselves in this image…."[5]

THE MYTH-MAKING MACHINE OF SOCIAL MEDIA

Today, we are all myth-makers. On Facebook, Instagram, and other platforms, we carefully curate personal mythologies—idealized representations of our lives. As Stephen West notes, "It becomes sort of like a museum dedicated to the person they want other people to think they are."[6] We post photos of hikes, brunches, and travels while omitting the mundane or unpleasant moments. Social media becomes a stage where we strive to appear exceptional, emulating the celebrity myths we see daily.

Unlike ancient myths, which invited reflection, today's celebrity culture sends the message that these figures are inherently superior to us. We obsess over every detail of their lives and seek their opinions on matters beyond their expertise—because we believe what they say must matter. (Hello, Bono!)

Modern myths also shape our everyday habits and consumption. Beer commercials, for example, suggest that drinking enhances social experiences, yet they omit the consequences of alcohol. Similarly, advertising convinces us we need gender-specific shampoos or deodorants. As Barthes pointed out, even soap can carry hidden messages about class and gender expectations.

Rather than rejecting myths, we must learn to engage with and reinterpret them. As Karen Armstrong argues:

> We need myths that will help us to identify with all our fellow-beings, not simply with those who belong to our ethnic, national or ideological tribe. We need myths that help us to realize the importance of compassion, which is not always regarded as sufficiently productive or efficient in our pragmatic, rational world. We need myths that help us to create a spiritual attitude, to see beyond our immediate requirements, and enable us to experience a transcendent value that challenges our solipsistic selfishness.[7]

The beauty of myths lies in their flexibility. Like Shakespeare's plays, myths can be adapted to suit new contexts and audiences. Lewis Klahr's films exemplify this reinterpretation. Klahr draws on mid-20th-century pop culture—comic books, science fiction, and advertisements—treating these cultural artifacts as his Greek myths.

A fascination with mythology seeps through almost all of Klahr's films. Beyond the direct and indirect references to Greek myths in the series Sixty-*Six* (2002–2015) and in shorts like *Alcestis* (2021), Klahr's explorations of mid-20th-century U.S. culture—through iconic L.A. landscapes, film noir, melodrama, comic books, science fiction, pop music, and even advertisements—serve as nods to modern mythologies. For Klahr, the seductive images of mid-20th-century pop culture and mass media are his Greek myths. These are the myths he was raised on. It wasn't Zeus, Mercury, or Aphrodite—it was Superman, Frank Sinatra, and those lush Vincent Minnelli melodramas.

Myths give us the illusion that we can comprehend existence and that we are not alone. While this can be problematic when taken too literally, sometimes an illusion is necessary to navigate chaos. As Klahr says, "Myths can be useful by helping us encapsulate the world, compressing and summarizing our understanding—or what we believe we understand—into a coherent form. And like most phenomena, they hold the potential for both good and evil, and every shade of gray in between."[8]

Klahr's interest in mythology dates back to his childhood. He recalls that it struck him profoundly from a very young age—around second or third grade—when he was introduced to it through Edith Hamilton's classic book. The fantasy within it was immediately appealing and pleasurable, resonating with him deeply.

In his 20s, Klahr encountered Robert Graves' seminal book, *The Greek Myths*:

> There were these half-page descriptions of the actual myths, followed by pages and pages of footnotes explaining what was buried inside these stories. They were incredibly compressed. I remember one footnote that described a single line as signifying the moment when the patriarchy took over from the matriarchy. And I just thought, 'Wow, such a huge change represented by just one line?' That seemed wildly and ecstatically poetic. Compression has always struck me as a vital element of narrative and history—what gets selected and how it's selected. How a sense of "lived time" is accumulated.[9]

Klahr's intention is neither to preserve Greek myths nor to demythologize them. Instead, he views them as:

> Endlessly useful and applicable; they never go out of style. Their openness ensures a flexibility of interpretation. They don't need me to keep them alive, as they are always present in some form and known worldwide. They also don't require demythologizing, since they are not dominant cultural forces like contemporary religions, social mores, or political ideologies that demand loyalty and subservience. They are simply available and do not need me to stay faithful to them out of fear of desecration, making them ripe for various adaptive uses.[10]

Klahr navigates the complex relationship with modern myths—superheroes, science fiction stories, pop music, and Hollywood cinema—by revisiting them through his work while simultaneously liberating them from the sometimes repressive chains of their original contexts. In his creative process, he essentially "heists" these materials, engaging in a two-part act of deconstruction. First, he physically cuts and removes images and objects from their original contexts, severing them from the sources of their power. Then, he uses these fragments to expose the illusion behind their influence, pulling back the curtain on their supposed authority. Often, as in *Pony Glass* (1997) and *Altair* (1995), for example, he imposes his own fictions upon these works, creating new possibilities. At the same time, Klahr, the archeologist, dives into the past to try to comprehend his—and our—present. In films like *Altair* and *Pony Glass*, Klahr tinkers with mythological consumer images and comic books, respectively, to craft new fictions that challenge the often restrictive and misleading myths of the originals.

In *Altair*, we are presented with the captivating mid-20th-century imagery of bars, drinks, and party life. However, the film reveals a deeper narrative: a woman's isolation and downfall. It explores themes of desire and our endless, often futile quest for fulfillment and recognition—symbolized by the title's reference to the brightest star. The allure of happiness and escape suggested by these images is ultimately exposed as illusory.

Klahr states:

> The film's montage guides the audience through various states of desire and attraction, plus social and legal complications, ultimately revealing the protagonist as 'a lonely woman with a drinking problem.' This depiction marks the end of her narrative arc within the film's timeframe. However, the starting point of her story—the seductiveness and glamor of drink and nightlife—is just as impactful and convincing as the film's conclusion. It is

Altair

> accurate to describe *Altair*'s narrative arc as moving from an idealization of alcohol to the debunking of its myth of joy, ultimately exposing the harsh consequences of overindulgence. Of course, *Altair* presents an elliptical narrative, making it challenging for many viewers to fully grasp the protagonist's progression.[11]

In *Pony Glass*, Klahr subverts the simplistic and idealized portrayals often found in comic books by focusing on Jimmy Olsen, Superman's nerdy and somewhat inconsequential sidekick. Through Olsen's journey of self-discovery and sexuality, Klahr transforms the character from a mere supporting role into a profound exploration of identity. For Klahr, Olsen functions as a bridge to Superman and his mythos, offering a relatable entry point for readers who might have felt overshadowed or marginalized by the superhero's overwhelming power. "By identifying with Jimmy," adds Klahr, "these readers could envision themselves as Superman's closest friend, thereby finding their own place within the superhero narrative."[12]

Klahr maintains that:

> Jimmy was pretty complicated. Part of what made him complicated is that DC Comics stories at this time weren't concerned with an ongoing continuity of a larger, coherent narrative, unlike the Marvel approach to their fictive universe. Their stories were standalone, leading to a kind of jungle of continuity paradoxes as they accumulated. This is also true of Greek mythology, where competing versions of various myths coexist. What I love about Greek mythology is that, instead of validating one version as the absolute truth, all versions are considered true.[13]

While altering the themes and context of the original images, Klahr retains the joy these comics brought him as a child, crafting stories that resonate with an adult audience. By "heisting" DC Comics, Klahr introduces themes of identity and sexuality—areas that were seldom explored in a meaningful way in the original comic books:

> What I'm doing with Jimmy in *Pony Glass* is placing him in a more mature world. In the comic book images that inspired the film, his cross-dressing as a woman was presented as an undercover disguise used for detective work to catch a gangster. In *Pony Glass*, however, Jimmy's motivation is transformed. Instead of using cross-dressing as a mere disguise, he is portrayed as a closeted man who uses it as a means to come out and embrace his homosexuality.[14]

In a sense, Klahr is reviving these characters and images, rescuing them from the often superficial portrayal found in comic books and the repressive attitudes of their time. This repression extended beyond comics; it reflected the broader mid-20th-century culture, where sexuality was rarely explored openly, and such topics were seldom discussed. As Klahr has mentioned, his intention is not to discredit existing stories or myths but to add a new layer

Pony Glass

of interpretation, creating another variation on the theme. As Barthes wrote, "Truth to tell, the best weapon against myth is perhaps to mythify it in its turn, and to produce an artificial myth and this reconstituted myth will in fact be a mythology. Since myth robs language of something, why not rob myths?"[15]

Klahr explores myths more directly in the series, *Sixty-Six* and the short work, *Alcestis* (part of *The Blue Rose of Forgetfulness* series). The roots of the project go back to 2009 when Klahr made the short, *Lethe*. This marked the first time that he combined mid-20th-century imagery with Greek myth:

> It became clear to me how I could construct my own versions of these stories. Before and during the making of that film, I read another deeply inspiring mythology book called *The Marriage of Cadmus and Harmony*

> by Roberto Calasso. It contained all these fantastic fragments and descriptions that would spin off in my imagination. *Helen of T* is a name I'd already come up with for a character for an unfinished short story I was working on, but there is a whole chapter about Helen of Troy in the Calasso book where he describes what she's like as a girl, the first time she's abducted, when she loses her virginity, and her marriage in the afterlife—all these things I never read or heard about before. So Calasso got me thinking.[16]

In *Sixty-Six*, Klahr takes Greek myths and characters, and dresses them up in 20th-century mass media imagery. The year 1966 was pivotal for Klahr: it marked his tenth birthday and the beginning of the "myths" of his life—comic books, pop music, and Hollywood genre films. "In *Sixty-Six*," Klahr reflects, "I was thinking that the mid-1960s imagery and era I was still enamored of was now so ancient in terms of my own lifespan that it was analogous to classic Greek mythology for me personally."[17]

Sixty-Six consists of 12 films or chapters, each representing a month of the calendar year. Some of the films, such as *Mercury*, *Erigone's Daughter*, *Saturn's Diary*, and *Lethe*, directly reference Greek characters and myths. Others, like *Ichor*, *Helen of T*, *Silver Age*, *Lip Print (Venus)*, and *Ambrosia*, are more loosely connected to these mythological themes. In *Orphacles*, Klahr ventures further, creating an entirely original myth.

As is typical in Klahr's work, *Sixty-Six* carries a prevailing sense of melancholy and disconnect. The characters—seemingly drawn from a mix of comic books, Hollywood melodramas, and film noirs—feverishly search across primarily Los Angeles landscapes for something elusive. Themes of identity and aging permeate many of the films within the series. Imagine blending a touch of Vincente Minnelli, a hint of Douglas Sirk, a dash of Greek mythology, and the iconic landscapes of Los Angeles—you'll end up with something reminiscent of *Sixty-Six*.

Klahr sequenced *Sixty-Six*, as he does with all his series, much like crafting a record album. Each film functions as a distinct song, carefully arranged according to various elements, such as tone, rhythm, theme, and color. Klahr explains, "I look for a sense of continuity and difference, just as I do when montaging a sequence of shots within an individual film. I aim to maintain a fresh, forward-moving flow that accumulates and builds as it progresses."[18]

In some ways, *Sixty-Six* works like a soap opera (or "call and response," says Klahr), taking us back and forth between different stories and themes. That said, you can find strong links between the different films. The opening "song," *Mercury*, and the later *Mars Garden* feel like companion pieces, not merely because they use a similar lightbox technique but also because they touch upon themes of masculinity.

Mercury is a melancholic vignette set to Leonard Cohen's somber yet hopeful "Minute Prologue." The soundtrack plays over overlapping comic book pages, depicting a meeting between two Flash characters from different eras (one of whom, with his helmet, resembles interpretations of Mercury). What unfolds from there is open to interpretation. Is it a greeting to the viewer? A depiction of Mercury, the messenger, racing by to escort us to the underworld that awaits us all? Or perhaps a dialogue between the young and old Flashes? Klahr's rapid in-camera movements, overlapping images, and blurred texts leave the interpretation to us, but a sense of time passing undeniably seeps through the rapid-fire imagery.

Drawing on Mars, the god of war, as a starting point, Klahr explores themes of masculinity in crisis in *Mars Garden*. Employing the same technique as in *Mercury*, Klahr uses a lightbox to create a collision between two pages of a comic book. Possibly seen through the fragmented memories of a man—emphasized by the final line, "I can't remember a thing"—we encounter blurred, overlapping images of archetypal businessmen and superheroes. This layering creates a ghostly sense of alter-egos and conflicting identities. Furthermore, the layering and framing suggest men who are constrained and trapped by societal expectations and pressures.

Once again, as seen in works like *Pony Glass*, Klahr liberates these characters from binary constraints by probing questions of identity and gender.

The second film in the series, *Ichor*, is the first of an informal quartet that includes *Saturn's Diary* and *The Silver Age*, and the fictional myth, *Orphacles*. Each of these films is linked by male protagonists seemingly struggling with a sense of self. *Ichor* refers to the golden fluid said to

Ichor

flow through the veins of gods and immortals, toxic to humans. With this idea as a backdrop, Klahr crafts a mysterious, alienated world populated by doctors, cops, corpses, red-haired women, blondes, and a man in a red suit.

There's no clear narrative—only a voice warning us to "beware of red-haired people" and a declaration that "by traveling eastward, you will gain; westward, you will lose. You will travel in both directions." No matter where we go, the voice seems to suggest, we'll find the same destination.

The color red dominates the film, suggesting illness, desire, and perhaps even murder. It's a thriller, a melodrama, and a meditation on mortality. This is where Klahr's impossible love affair with mid-20th-century America becomes evident. It's a utopia that never existed, yet he can't help but long for it. His comic book characters resemble gods but are, in reality, mere humans—just cutouts.

In a different vein, *Saturn's Diary* sees Klahr revisiting themes of masculinity—specifically through the figure of a ladies' man—embodied by Saturn, the god of time. Saturn bears a resemblance to Gene Barry, the actor from the TV show *Burke's Law*, from which the comic images are drawn. The narrative unfolds over the first four months of Saturn's life in 1966, though these months reveal little of substance. In fact, he struggles to remember entire days. Saturn is depicted as the archetypal 1960s suit-and-tie man, caught in a monotonous routine of appointments, work, washing, TV static, smoking, and drinking. While he projects the image of a suave ladies' man, beneath this façade lies a profoundly lonely individual with little emotional

The Silver Age

depth. Eventually, he fades from the screen, replaced by flat colors and fragmented landscapes, symbolizing how his dullness has rendered him invisible.

The Silver Age unfolds as a fragmented narrative, accompanied by backward love songs, which not only underscore the retrospective nature of the events but also hint at the characters' sense of entrapment in the past. Throughout this journey, we encounter familiar figures from the previous films: the man in the red suit, the enigmatic doctors, and Saturn himself.

In *Ichor*, there was a palpable sense that a crime or an act of violence had occurred. The evidence was subtle but unmistakable—empty safe boxes and the ominous presence of a gun. These clues pointed to something significant, yet the exact nature of the event remained elusive, leaving the viewer with an unsettling sense of incompleteness:

> Before *The Silver Age*, I had employed my characters—which I'd culled from a comic book created from a '60s TV show called *Burke's Law*—to evoke a sense of mundane everyday life, but with very little reference to criminal activity. In *The Silver Age* I activated my characters' crime-story origins primarily by including a series of open-doored and empty, looted safes.[19]

The film culminates in a final scene where we briefly see a man and a bottle with an image of Mercury on it. The presence of Mercury, the messenger god, raises the question: is he there to guide the man to the underworld, or is his appearance symbolic of a deeper, more metaphorical journey?

Orphacles is another daytime noir. This time, Klahr creates his own mythical characters—though some will be recognizable from *Ichor* and *Saturn's Diary*. "Oprhacles was just a word/name that popped into my head while I was making 66," says Klahr. "I guess it's a splice of Orpheus and Herakles though the film I made has nothing to do with either of those 2 characters. judging by what I did create in this film, this character seems to be an embodiment of rage."

While not directly linked to the *Ichor*, *Saturn*, and *Silver Age* trilogy, *Orphacles* acts as a casual companion and a bookend to this informal trilogy. The film weaves together elements of hypnosis, the Hotel Fremont, mysterious phone calls, planes, and a body being carried out of an equally enigmatic bungalow. It all builds up to an intense climax involving an insect infecting a man. The backdrop resembles a twisted game of Twister, and as the man flees and exits the bungalow, he encounters another body—perhaps an old one. Is this a conflict of masculinity? The sensitive poet versus the so-called muscular man? Klahr might be suggesting that the ideal man is not one or the other but rather a complex intersection of sensitivity, compassion, and strength.

Amid these lush films lie two anomalies, deeply autobiographical works that reflect Klahr's personal mythologies from his youth: *August 19, 1966 (Jupiter Sends a Message)* and *Ambrosia*. Klahr explains:

> I had to consciously decide whether to include them. I ultimately chose to do so because they encapsulate the time period and broaden the reach and scope of the series as a whole. They also offer a different engagement that isn't character-driven.[20]

August 19, 1966 (Jupiter Sends a Message) opens with a chorus of cricket sounds piercing the air on a hot summer day. The scene is filled with drinks, cars, and socializing—a snapshot of suburban life. Travel plans are evident: floral bed sheets, suitcases, and scattered branches evoke the remnants of a summer long gone. As clouds gather, distant thunder rumbles, signaling a shift in the atmosphere.

A silent companion of sorts to *August 19, 1966, Ambrosia* unfolds as another personal myth. Black-and-white photos (taken from Klahr's older brother's Bar Mitzvah and also used in Album) capture a banquet hall in the aftermath of a feast of the gods. We see only the remnants: dirty plates, glasses, empty bottles, and scattered chairs. The party is over, the gods have fled, and the mess is all that remains.

Both films are reminiscent of Robert Pollard's rough lo-fi short songs that often break up the longer, more polished pieces on Guided by Voices records. Unlike the other films, these ones delve headfirst into personal mythology, with Klahr reflecting on a memorable summer from his childhood that inspired August 19, 1966:

> There were these five super humid days in late August [1966] when a summer thunderstorm was threatening but wouldn't arrive. My best friend was away on vacation with his family. My mother, perceiving my loneliness, treated me with extra special kindness and love– her love was rarely that explicit. I knew my mother loved me, that wasn't the issue, but she was particularly effusive over those five days. And I remember at one point she sent me off to the toy store to buy a Matchbox Car, even though it wasn't time for my allowance. It was just an extra special gift that she was giving me. But even then I understood that the gift wasn't what was important, it was the love she was expressing. So that's all wrapped up in the film.[21]

Finally, we come to a series of films featuring female protagonists who grapple with loneliness, aging, sexuality, identity, and generational conflict.

In *Helen of T*, a sudden burst of jazzy noir horns over the sound of traffic immediately places us in an urban cityscape. Chain-smoking Helen walks the streets alone. She's no great beauty—Klahr describes her as "more Helen

Helen of T

of Troy, New York," a kind of low-rent bar girl. Klahr's Helen roams the city streets and lives alone in her apartment, smoking and waiting for a call that never comes.

In part two, Helen has aged significantly. Not much has changed; she still lives alone, now with her instant dinners. Throughout the film, blurred fragments come and go like fleeting memories, struggling desperately to be recalled. There's an overwhelming sense of loneliness and emptiness. Once "lovely," Helen is now wrinkled and alone, with only fading time, instant dinners, a lighter (fittingly named Prometheus), and her wilted flowers for company.

Channeling the playful symbolism of Douglas Sirk with the visual elegance of Vincente Minnelli, Klahr offers a profoundly humanized portrayal of the Helen of Troy myth.

In mythology, Erigone was the daughter of Icarius, who met a tragic fate at the hands of Dionysus. Upon discovering her father's body, Erigone hanged herself in despair. In Klahr's reimagining, *Erigone's Daughter* is transformed into a young blonde protagonist reminiscent of Tippi Hedren in Alfred Hitchcock's *Marnie* or *The Birds*. This version is constructed from 1970s Portuguese Foto Roman characters, set against a backdrop of audio snippets from the classic 1960s TV show *Route 66*—a subtle nod to both the title and the iconic American highway.

Erigone's Daughter

In this retelling, Erigone is portrayed as a young woman who may or may not have a drug problem but is clearly at odds with the older generation. She appears to seek out hired men for some unknown job and returns to her childhood home to relocate her mother's gravesite. Klahr might be envisioning the life of Icarius' widow, who perhaps died young in an alcohol-related incident. Alternatively, this troubled Erigone may be seeking a burial plot for herself, with the men she hired intended to kill her. Regardless, it's evident that something dramatic has occurred, as the small town she returns to seems to shun her and her family. Yet, as Erigone cryptically states, "what I really remember" remains elusive.

Lip Print (Venus) finds Klahr panning, zooming, and darting across romance comic book pages to the strains of Debussy's *Clair de Lune* in this mini-melodrama—think mini-rock opera—depicting a blonde woman, Venus, the goddess of love, as she grapples with her desires. Faces shift in and out, capturing fleeting glances and gestures. Unheard phone calls add to the sense of longing. A mysterious brunette appears. Could she, rather than the men, be the true object of Venus' desires?

Concluding *Sixty-Six* is the film that sparked Klahr's interest in Greek myth films: *Lethe* (2009).

In mythology, Lethe is the underworld river where the dead drink to erase the memories of their past lives. It symbolizes rebirth and the ability to start anew, free from the burdens of the past.

In Klahr's sci-fi/melodrama update, two scientists work on a concoction designed to make a man younger. After taking the injection, the man

Lethe

transforms into a somewhat younger version of himself. The appearance of wet undergarments suggests a rebirth of bedroom activities, but things quickly take a strange turn. The woman involved seems confused by their actions. While the man can regain youth, she is left questioning her own place in this transformation. Ultimately, the attempt at rebirth leads only to grotesque accidents, anguish, and loss.

Klahr explores themes of our attempts to recapture the past and recover lost youth. While the idea of returning to a previous state may seem appealing, he underscores the risk that clinging to the past can cause us to lose touch with the present—and, ultimately, with ourselves.

Although *Alcestis* was included in the later series *The Blue Rose of Forgetfulness*, it could easily have fit into *Sixty-Six* alongside the female-led films and was something Klahr considered.

The original tale of Alcestis unfolds like this: Alcestis, the daughter of King Pelias, is sought after by many suitors. Her father decrees that the first man to harness a boar and a lion to a chariot will win her hand. Admetus succeeds, but only with the help of the god Apollo. Soon after their marriage, Admetus discovers snakes in his bed—a sign of his impending death. Apollo, having intoxicated the Fates, persuades them to allow someone else to die in Admetus's place. Eventually, Alcestis agrees to sacrifice herself. Later, Heracles rescues her from the underworld.

In Klahr's loose adaptation, the story is set at a house party, and Apollo is reimagined as a gardener with a prominent "dong" who has the power to create gold. As the plot unfolds, Alcestis finds herself in the underworld, where she appears to relish her time with multiple lovers. Pollux, a lover from her previous life, is among them, but her primary companions are animal-headed figures—especially the Tiger—who serve as Pluto's assistants. Her time in the underworld ends when Heracles arrives to retrieve her. However, upon returning, Alcestis finds that Admetus is now with another woman. She is left alone to raise their three children.

Klahr's fusion of 1950s Hollywood melodramas with Greek myths may seem unusual but is surprisingly fitting. Almost every Greek myth involves domestic chaos: a man, a woman, in-laws, and children, all entangled in desire, adultery, lust, and murder. In this context, *Lethe* might represent Klahr's ideal synthesis of collage, 20th-century aesthetics, and Greek mythology.

At the heart of *Sixty-Six* and *Alcestis* lie trouble and desire. Feckless characters navigate mysterious and often deserted urban environments in search of something they can't quite define—because they don't fully know what they're looking for, and what they might be seeking has already long gone. Klahr loosely draws on myths to explore themes of identity, alienation, and aging. There's a sense of restlessness in many of the characters and a pervasive societal malaise.

Like David Lynch in *Blue Velvet* or *Twin Peaks*, Klahr takes us beneath the lush, seductive mythological exteriors to reveal an existential sickness—a society that has lost its way, its sense of right and wrong, and ultimately, its sense of self.

For Klahr, the appeal of myth is that it provides a bridge to older traditions yet can't quite be called history, "It's more like fictions that are useful, or long-lasting, elemental," Klahr said in a 2016 interview with *Cinema Scope*. "They are competing versions of stories which all contain partial or paradoxical truth—in a sense, everything is true, so there's a great openness and adaptability to these texts."[22]

Myths are free-flowing and eternal. They arrive, change, disappear, and are reborn. Myth distorts, yet it can also lead us to a deeper truth than any amount of facts can reveal. The danger lies in our inability to see the form and instead focus solely on the meaning. For Klahr and Barthes, the key is looking beyond the meaning to the form. We must distance ourselves from the message to see how it has been formed. It's like watching a landscape through the window of a moving car, unaware of the windowpane that moderates the view. Though present, the pane is at once absent.

Klahr's myth-drenched films (and I've only touched upon a handful) are an album of melancholy and disillusionment. It could be argued that they are about the failures of myths. He takes us to a world where the myths we once believed in seem to have let us down. The gods, the people we admired—they have failed us. We're left alone with the pieces, alone with each other.

Maybe that's not a bad thing.

NOTES

1 Roland Barthes, *Mythologies*. New York: Hill and Wang, 2013, p. 240.
2 Karen Armstrong, *A Short History of Myth*. Edinburgh: Canongate Books Ltd., 2005, p. 51.
3 Armstrong, *A Short History of Myth*, p. 1.
4 https://www.philosophizethis.org/podcast/structuralism-and-mythology-pt-1
5 Barthes, *Mythologies*, p. 270.
6 https://www.philosophizethis.org/podcast/structuralism-and-mythology-pt-2
7 Armstrong, *A Short History of Myth*, p. 52.
8 Email exchange with Author, March 2024.
9 https://cinema-scope.com/cinema-scope-magazine/era-extrana-lewis-klahr-sixty-six/
10 Email exchange with the Author, March 2024.
11 Email exchange with the Author, March 2024.
12 Email exchange with the Author, March 2024.
13 Email exchange with the Author, March 2024.
14 Email exchange with the Author, March 2024.
15 Barthes, *Mythologies*, pp. 246–247.
16 https://cinema-scope.com/cinema-scope-magazine/era-extrana-lewis-klahr-sixty-six/
17 Email exchange with Author, March 2024.
18 Email exchange with Author, March 2024.
19 https://cinema-scope.com/cinema-scope-magazine/era-extrana-lewis-klahr-sixty-six/
20 Email exchange with Author, August 2024.
21 https://chicagoreader.com/blogs/lewis-klahrs-sixty-six-is-a-masterful-journey-through-inner-space-and-the-american-past/
22 https://cinema-scope.com/cinema-scope-magazine/era-extrana-lewis-klahr-sixty-six/

Bad Love Is Easy to Do

4

In Lewis Klahr's worlds, love, lust, desire, flirtation, sex, and romance—regardless of the label—are depicted as messy and complicated. In series such as *Engram Sepals*, *The Couplets*, *The Rain Couplets*, and *Blue Rose of Forgetfulness*, love appears deceitful, volatile, orgasmic, heartbreaking, and, at times, even beautiful. This portrayal contrasts sharply with the neat, idealized myths sold to us by Hollywood films, romance novels, and love songs. Klahr's depiction suggests that love is often fragmented, inconsistent, and fleeting—far from the tidy narratives we are conditioned to expect.

Klahr's use of appropriated materials from pop culture, advertising, and mass media emphasizes this complexity. His characters, objects, and settings—cutouts from comic books, magazines, and advertisements—reflect a world shaped by consumerism and capitalism. Through these elements, Klahr suggests that we have become so preoccupied with collecting material possessions and distractions, convincing ourselves that they will enhance our health, status, and lives, that we lose sight of both each other and ourselves. Most of us live according to the dominant ideology—how we walk, dress, think, eat, watch, read, and exist—all guided by prevailing trends and market demands.

But what exactly is love? Even in the 20th and 21st centuries of capitalism and hyper-consumerism, are we loving the right way? To explore these

Pony Glass

DOI: 10.1201/9781003427223-4

questions, let's turn to a few philosophers—individuals with plenty to say on the matter.

Well, let's go back to the beginnings and Plato (whose name inspired a phrase he never uttered: platonic love). In Plato's fictional work, *The Symposium* (fancy word for dinner party) a bunch of hungover famous guys (Socrates, Aristophanes, etc.) get together and take turns defining what love entails.

Aristophanes, the comedic playwright, presents an absurd yet profound allegory. He imagines a time when humans were originally fused together: two heads, four arms, and four legs, rolling through the world in spherical forms. There were three sexes—male, female, and androgynous—each descended from celestial bodies: males from the sun, females from the earth, and androgynous beings from the moon. When these beings grew rebellious and sought to challenge the gods, Zeus split them in half. This division, Aristophanes explains, left humans forever searching for their "other half," striving to restore the original wholeness they lost.

As bizarre as Aristophanes' account may seem, it aligns with certain modern psychological theories. Jacques Lacan's concept of the mirror stage describes how, early in life, children perceive themselves as united with the world. However, upon seeing their reflection, they realize they are separate individuals. This moment triggers a lifelong pursuit of an impossible wholeness, often sought through love or consumerism—neither of which can truly fulfill it.

This idea echoes in everyday phrases uttered by lovers, "You complete me" or "You're my soulmate." Yet, as romantic as these sentiments may sound, they reflect an illusion—no other person can make us whole. True wholeness, as countless philosophers suggest, must come from within.

Okay, back to Plato. Returning to *The Symposium*, Socrates offers a different perspective. While he agrees that love is a pursuit, he contends that it's not about recovering a missing part of ourselves but about seeking beauty and goodness. Drawing on a conversation with Diotima—a possibly fictional figure—Socrates explains that love progresses in stages. It begins with an attraction to physical beauty and evolves toward a deeper appreciation of the soul. Over time, love transcends physical desire, revealing that true connection lies in the meeting of minds and personalities.

Later philosophical movements, especially Romanticism, built on this idea, proposing that love involves emotional intensity and the pursuit of a soulmate. However, not all philosophers agreed with this idealized view.

Grumpy ol' Arthur Schopenhauer, for instance, offered a far more cynical interpretation. He compared romantic relationships to two porcupines seeking warmth—needing each other but wary of getting too close to avoid being hurt. For Schopenhauer, love is less about unity and more about survival. He argued that romantic attraction is not rooted in genuine affection but driven by an unconscious instinct to find a partner whose traits complement our weaknesses. Love, according to Schopenhauer, is an irrational impulse designed to further reproduction, often causing people to make poor decisions in the throes of passion.

Schopenhauer even likened marriage to blindly reaching into a sack of snakes, warning that love often leads to unpredictable and disappointing outcomes. He argued that many people mistakenly equate love with happiness, believing that falling in love will bring lifelong fulfillment. However, Schopenhauer cautioned that love and happiness are distinct—and one does not guarantee the other. Love, in his view, is merely a tool—an overwhelming emotion that convinces rational beings to act irrationally in the service of reproduction, not lasting joy.

Erich Fromm, writing in his 1956 book *The Art of Loving*, focused on the problem of human separateness. He argued that humans, aware of their isolation in the vastness of the universe, experience profound existential loneliness. To alleviate this isolation, people seek connections—often through love. As Fromm observes:

> They are starved for [love]; they watch endless numbers of films about happy and unhappy love stories, they listen to hundreds of trashy songs about love—yet hardly anyone thinks that there is anything that needs to be learned about love.[1]

Fromm believed that in modern capitalist societies, love becomes transactional—a product to be consumed. He described this phenomenon as the "personality market," where individuals offer themselves as commodities, hoping to fulfill each other's insecurities. This commodified form of love is fleeting and ultimately unsatisfying. As Fromm explains:

> Modern man's happiness consists in the thrill of looking at the shop windows, and in buying all that he can afford to buy, either for cash or on installments. He (or she) looks at people in a similar way.[2]

In this transactional view of love, attractiveness is equated with success and popularity. Men and women seek partners not for true connection but based on their market value—settling for the best available option, much like buying a house. Fromm argued that traits such as wealth, power, and prestige are often prioritized over genuine love.

For Fromm, true love is not a passive experience but an active choice and a skill that requires cultivation. Love, he insisted, should not be treated as an object to be acquired but as a dynamic process—a verb centered on fostering the growth and happiness of others, regardless of whether they meet our personal needs. To love authentically, one must first learn to be comfortable alone, free from the ego's tendency to use others for personal gain.

Fromm viewed love as an art form, demanding effort, patience, and objectivity. He believed that only by loving universally—rather than selectively—can we transcend our separateness and build meaningful connections. However, in a society that glorifies success, prestige, money, and power, embracing this kind of love requires a countercultural mind-set. Genuine love demands objectivity and resists the temptation to restrict affection only to those deemed worthy, for doing so undermines the very essence of love.

Why explore these philosophical perspectives? The point is to highlight that love is a complex, messy endeavor—one that many of us misunderstand or get wrong. Much of what we've been sold as "love" is, as discussed in the previous chapter, a myth—a neatly packaged Hollywood fantasy marketed to us repeatedly.

Isn't that exactly what capitalism thrives on? Every commercial promises that some product will make your life better, solve your problems, or even make you more lovable. But, of course, it's all nonsense.

Hollywood films, romance novels, and pop songs construct a simplistic narrative about love and romance, stripping away the contradictions, conflicts, and absurdities. Real love, as Klahr portrays it, is far messier. It is unpredictable, occasionally ugly, and often violent—infinitely more nuanced than the sanitized stories mass media presents.

Lewis Klahr acknowledges that his transformation of materials:

> often involves moving away from the clichés and stereotypes of gender and sexual representation—exaggerations common in most of the drawing styles—and grounding them in something closer to experiences I've had or observed in people I know, providing a sense of realism. The lack of closure fits with this approach, as I find the world filled with ambiguity and multiple meanings, often contradictory.[3]

Klahr's love of melodrama—especially the works of Vincente Minnelli and, to a lesser extent, Douglas Sirk—pervades much of his filmography. Like these sweeping, emotional melodramas, Klahr's narratives are saturated with heightened emotions and unresolved tensions.

Recurring themes of longing, lust, and desire drive his work. His characters often struggle to connect—with others, with themselves, and with the world—resulting in a persistent sense of disconnection and alienation. By repurposing vintage materials in his collages, Klahr adds an additional layer of meaning. His cutout figures exist in a fabricated fantasy of promise and hope, yet the world they inhabit always feels incomplete and unattainable.

His films evoke a sense of an endless chase—men pursuing women, women pursuing men, men pursuing men, and so on. Brief encounters do occur, but they are usually fleeting and unsatisfying.

Klahr also engages with the repression of past eras. His characters—*Pony Glass* being a notable example—are initially confined by the rigid societal norms of their time. However, within Klahr's stories, they experience new forms of liberation, indulging in sexual freedom with men and women alike. Yet even with this newfound freedom, intimacy remains awkward and mechanical. Characters go through the motions of passion, but genuine emotion feels absent or minimal. In *In the Months of Crickets* (1988), for instance, a severed head performs oral sex on a woman, as if suggesting that the body—and any deeper connection—has become irrelevant.

Klahr explains:

> Part of the impulse I described—collage as a way to live many lives—comes from my identity as a narrative filmmaker more than an experimental one. The narrative genre is where I feel most at home. While many commercial films use violence to heighten dramatic conflict, that never interested me much. What fascinates me is how sex and love relate to people's development of their identities, and that's something I never grow tired of. Pop music is the same with its endless love songs.[4]

One of Klahr's earliest explorations of love—particularly obsessive love—is *Her Fragrant Emulsion* (1987), a collage of fragmented film strips featuring B-movie actress Mimsy Farmer. The film unfolds like a distorted striptease: ruptured images of Farmer move awkwardly across the screen, evoking an impossible pursuit—a desire destined to remain unfulfilled. Her face flickers, shifting in and out of the frame, offering brief moments of intimacy that vanish just as quickly. It mirrors the fleeting intoxication of young love, with its ephemeral honeymoon phase. No matter how intensely Klahr pursues her image, the Mimsy Farmer of his imagination is fated to remain trapped in the shadows of time and space.

Klahr's fascination with Farmer began in the spring of 1978, after he saw Barbet Schroeder's film *More* (1969). "That's when I began tracking down different movies she'd been in," Klahr recalls.

> She does a marvelous LSD dance in *Riot on Sunset Strip* (1967) after being doused by her male classmates, who then take turns gangbanging her. Mimsy's character suffers a similar fate in *Devil's Angels* (1967), though without the drugs. As I delved deeper into her filmography, I realized I'd seen her in a number of films growing up, but she hadn't left a lasting impression. In *More*, though, she had fully entered her countercultural femme fatale mode, luring the young protagonist into self-destructive hedonism, including heroin use that ultimately kills him.[5]

For *Her Fragrant Emulsion*, Klahr rephotographed images of Mimsy from *The Road to Salina* (1970), which he describes as "a kind of hippie noir amnesia story" starring Robert Walker Jr., Rita Hayworth, and Ed Begley Sr. "I used to watch it late at night on broadcast TV. To get a VHS of *The*

Road to Salina to rephotograph in Super 8, I had to track it down at a store in Times Square that specialized in out-of-print movies."[6]

In the Month of Crickets (part of the *Tales of The Forgotten Future* series, 1988–1991), composed of vintage black-and-white illustrations, advertising photos, and movie stills, is not a traditional love story. Instead, it alludes to a sequence of erotic encounters and murky affairs unfolding within a hotel. As expected, everything is far from black and white. The film resembles an ensemble piece, subverting the glossy, idealized portrayals of romance characteristic of old Hollywood.

A foggy night. The sound of crickets. A man and a woman arrive at a hotel. They visit bars and clubs. The man becomes infatuated with a dancer... crickets chirp... silence stretches. No one speaks. Despite being physically together, the characters remain emotionally distant. Affairs are implied—perhaps even escorts. Drinks, dancers, dining... hints of bribes, extortion, and murder linger. A man watches a woman undress while a photographer lurks unseen. The characters may change from scene to scene, but narrative continuity isn't the point. Instead, the film deconstructs ideas of romance and fidelity—everyone seems to be engaging in something, yet the encounters are fleeting, and intimacy is absent.

Despite the activity, a deep melancholy permeates the film. It feels like a bedroom farce with a twist: everyone is getting "it" (and often paying for "it"), yet there's a familiar sense of disconnect. As thinkers like Erich Fromm suggested, physical attraction only lasts so long before the pursuit of the next idealized body begins. But, in the end, there's no genuine connection, no love—just a repetitive cycle of lust and desire. A woman brushes a man's leg with her foot. A severed head performs oral sex on a woman, as if the body—and any deeper connection—has become irrelevant. A woman adjusts her fragmented face in a mirror. Stockings, shoes, and glimpses of incomplete bodies reinforce the characters' objectification. They exist as commodities in transactional exchanges, underscored by the lurking presence of a menacing photographer.

The film's whirlwind of characters is difficult to follow, perhaps intentionally—a reflection on the sameness of it all, with everyone chasing the same fleeting thrills. It's reminiscent of *Grand Hotel* (1932), but with a kinkier, more jaded edge.

In both *Cartoon Far* (1990) and *Elevator Music* (1991)—part of the *Mood Opulence* section of *Tales of the Forgotten Future*—Klahr explores two contrasting relationships. These films are among several where Klahr combines original cutout materials with cutout photos of live-action performances. For him, using actors provided more "control and continuity of character for storytelling. I was interested in being both more clear and staying as narratively suggestive as *In the Month of the Crickets* is."[7]

In *Cartoon Far*, the blonde woman and the race car driver are portrayed by Teresa Podlesney and Michael Krauss, respectively. The film's first half features the Shangri-Las' somber talk-song "Past, Present, and Future," itself a kind of collage, incorporating segments of Beethoven's *Moonlight Sonata*. The song speaks of "silent joys and broken toys," as the woman reflects on her tumultuous romance with the driver. In the second half, set to Percy Faith's cover of "The Look of Love," the driver seems to recount their relationship before his inevitable crash, spinning out of control toward his demise. The ambiguity lingers: did he intentionally end his life, or was the crash an accident that underscored the triviality of their quarrels?

Klahr's fusion of actors and collage in *Elevator Music* creates a jarring, surreal experience that mirrors the protagonist's fractured mental state. She engages in sexual acts with a man, represented through idealized illustrations. When he ghosts her, she drives through a seemingly perfect suburban neighborhood—depicted using mid-20th-century illustrations of smiling families, pristine homes, and immaculate lawns. Later, after much pill popping, she appears to participate in a chaotic orgy involving men, women, an ape, and a pirate (all portrayed as drawings), leaving viewers to question the film's reality. Did the man ever exist, or was he a figment of her troubled imagination?

The collage elements underscore the unrealistic expectations and fantasies cultivated by consumer culture—desires that can never be fully realized.

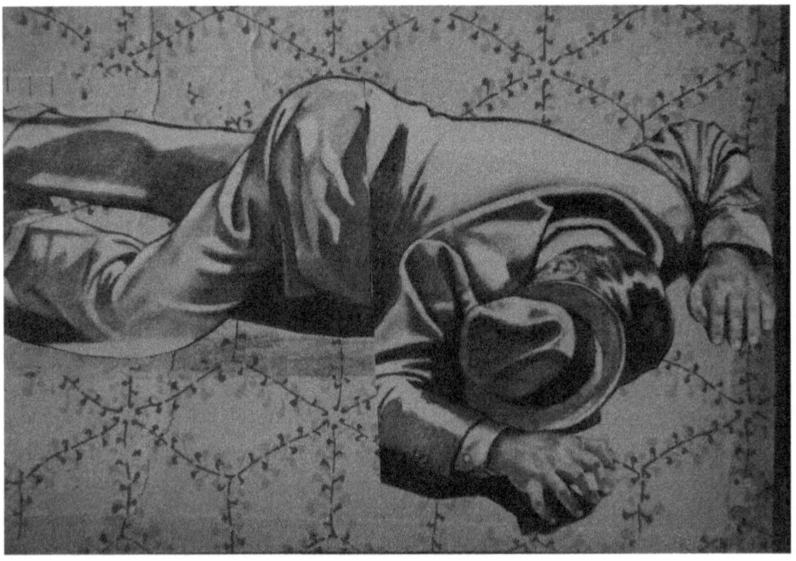

Engram Sepals

Engram Sepals is a series of melodramas inspired by Klahr's fascination with the Technicolor films of the 1950s. While not every film in the series centers on love, they all delve into the complexities, turbulence, beginnings, and endings of human relationships—particularly within the context of American culture. Klahr has described the series as a reflection of American intoxication, both through substances and romance, spanning from the 1940s to the 1970s. We've already discussed *Altair* and *Pony Glass*, both of which explore themes of love and desire, with characters searching for connection and a sense of identity. (*Elsa Kirk* was addressed earlier in the section on memory and mass media.)

In *Altair*, the female protagonist seems desperate for companionship but finds only empty jewelry boxes, fleeting affairs, and an excess of alcohol. Though she is wined and dined, she remains isolated, struggling to navigate a male-dominated world.

As Klahr explains:

> The images were culled from six late-forties issues of *Cosmopolitan* magazine and set to an almost four-minute segment of Stravinsky's *Firebird* (looped twice) to create a sinister, perfumed world. As in my 1988 visit to this genre in *In The Month of Crickets*, the narrative is highly smudged, leaving legible only the larger signposts of the female protagonist's story. The viewer is encouraged to speculate on the nature and details of the woman's battle with large, malevolent societal forces and her descent into an alcoholic swoon. However, it is important to note that all of the above was only discovered on the editing table. What motivated me during the shooting of this film, which was largely improvisatory, was a fascination with the color blue and some ineffable association it has for me with both California and what I imagined to be the great sense of relieved openness of the post-war 1940s.[8]

In *Pony Glass*, Klahr repurposes old comic book characters and magazine photos to explore Jimmy Olsen's inner turmoil. Haunted by his unspoken desire for Superman, Jimmy attempts to distract himself by pursuing a relationship with Lana, Lois Lane's sister. However, their growing connection does little to alleviate his sadness. Eventually, Jimmy embraces cross-dressing and discovers a preference for certain sexual experiences, leading to his acceptance of his homosexuality—or perhaps his bisexuality.

In the film's first act, an older Jimmy is shown sitting beside his wife. They do not appear happy, suggesting that continued self-denial may ultimately destroy him. As the narrative unfolds, a spherical device seems to manipulate Jimmy's thoughts. His dreams shift from Superman to women's clothing, and soon, he begins dressing as a woman and engaging in relationships with men. What begins as hypnosis or mind control ultimately reveals Jimmy's true self.

The title film, *Engram Sepals* (2000), draws on elements reminiscent of Billy Wilder's noir melodrama *Sunset Boulevard.* The title itself evokes the concept of memory traces. The film opens with a haunting image: a dead man lying on a rug. From this unsettling beginning, viewers are presented with fragmented, puzzle-like details—elevator buttons (possibly suggesting the murderer's escape?), a mysterious woman, and the piercing glare of car headlights.

Klahr shifts between photographic scenes and white sketches of characters, which are ghostly and incomplete, existing in a liminal state—like spirits in purgatory or hell. Some sketches resemble the eerie, otherworldly style of Gustave Doré, adding to the sense that these figures are lost between life and death. Or perhaps they represent fragmented memories, as a dying man struggles to grasp his fading recollections.

Klahr was drawn to these sketches because "the whites against blacks are so luminous that they have a kind of eternity in them."[9] These figures—neither fully alive nor dead—exist in limbo, suspended between two worlds. In the final shot, sketched hands reach out, attempting to guide the dead man into the afterlife.

It remains unclear what led the man to his tragic end. Was he ensnared in an affair? The scattered clues—glimpses of a home, a child, and a lover—are fragmented and distorted. There's even a suggestion of corporate espionage, as if personal and professional betrayals have merged into a single, fatal spiral. This seems to be yet another tale of broken love, where desire mutates into an insatiable hunger for more. Lust and greed, intertwined, become destructive forces, unraveling the man's life and dragging him toward his inevitable demise, leaving only echoes of his existence behind.

The remaining films—*Govinda* (1999), *Downs Are Feminine* (1993), and *A Failed Cardigan Maneuver* (1999)—explore themes of love, desire, connection, and identity.

Govinda features Super 8 home movie footage of a high school and a hippie wedding, accompanied by a Hare Krishna mantra and The Stooges' "We Will Fall." The film is a three-act meditation on the rise and fall of American counterculture in the 1960s and 1970s, tracing a journey from idealism to disillusionment, followed by an attempt at reintegration. Klahr presents a generation in search of identity and fulfillment, echoing themes explored by thinkers like Schopenhauer and Fromm. Through sex, drugs, music, and dance, the characters explore life's possibilities, testing boundaries in search of meaning.

However, this period of uninhibited exploration inevitably ends, as adulthood, responsibility, and societal expectations intervene. The wedding symbolizes a bridge between youthful rebellion and the conventional life that follows, with former rebels settling beside their elders, who made similar transitions long ago. The film concludes with a melancholic tone, as wild, Dionysian behaviors give way to weddings, buffets, and subdued dancing.

Downs Are Feminine (named after the Mercury Rev song *Downs Are Feminine Balloons*) is a bold, uninhibited collage of eroticism, teetering on the edge of pornography. Love, romance, and desire are stripped down to raw, relentless sexual cravings. Gender boundaries blur—men have vaginas, women have penises, and even hand-penises appear. The film explores pill-popping and sexual encounters, both straight and queer, highlighting the extremes people pursue in their search for love and self-discovery.

In this world of fleeting pleasures—sex, drugs, and alcohol—characters seek everything but love, perhaps unaware that what they truly crave is connection. Klahr draws parallels between sexual encounters and consumerism, suggesting that we "fuck" the things we buy, chasing the same fleeting high from material objects as we do from physical intimacy. In one scene, a Grace Kelly stamp—symbolizing the pristine image of pop culture—stands in stark contrast to the messy reality beneath the surface, where purity is an illusion and excess reigns.

The series concludes with *A Failed Cardigan Maneuver*—a powerful three-song mini-melodrama. Klahr follows an everyman (representing a generation) from an idealized childhood, through the devastation of World War II, to the hollow corporate bachelor life of the 1950s—and perhaps toward a final glimmer of hope for meaningful love in old age.

The film opens with Gordon Jenkins' rendition of "Be Careful, It's My Heart," pairing nostalgic illustrations with idealized advertising imagery—a callback to *The Pharaoh's Belt*—to evoke the innocence of childhood. As the narrative shifts into adulthood, Sinatra's "One for My Baby" replaces the idyllic visions of youth with a darker, emptier world shaped by war, hunger, loneliness, soulless jobs, bars, and fleeting encounters with prostitutes. The bright promise of the future gives way to the harsh realities of adulthood in a cold, capitalist society.

The film concludes with Sinatra's "What's New," a melancholic reflection on reconnecting with an old flame. Now in the twilight of life, the character reflects on lost dreams and fading time. Yet, in the final scene, a woman enters his office, offering a glimmer of hope. Could this be the rekindling of lost love—a chance, after decades of shallow highs, for true intimacy and connection?

Through *Engram Sepals*, Klahr captures the alienation and disconnection pervasive in modern society. We are lost, searching for quick fixes—affairs, bars, casual sex, indulgence—only to find loneliness, aging, and mortality. We are conditioned to believe that satisfaction lies just beyond our reach, leaving us endlessly hungry for more.

Klahr's series *The Couplets* (2009–2010), *The Rain Couplets* (2012), and *Blue Rose of Forgetfulness* (2021) engage more explicitly with love, romance, desire, and the complexities that come with them.

April Snow

In *The Couplets*, each film pairs songs—or variations of a song—to explore the nuances of romance and love. Klahr explains:

> When I made mixtapes in the '80s, I was exploring ideas about montage and sequencing to create meaning. The first idea for a couplet came from a juxtaposition of two love songs I had put together on a mixtape after breaking up with an important girlfriend for the first but not the last time. This mix became the soundtrack for *April Snow.* I paired The Shangri-Las' *Out in the Streets*' with Springsteen's "*Racing in the Street*", which felt like an answer song. The difference was that the former had a female point of view, while the latter was from a male perspective.[10]

April Snow (2010) opens with "Out in the Street," establishing a "she said/he said" narrative. Through a blend of cutout drawings, photos, and illustrations, the female protagonist reflects on how her partner has changed since they first met. He combs his hair differently, acts unlike the man she fell in love with, and no longer finds joy in their relationship. Despite her love, guilt clouds her thoughts—she fears that their relationship has stifled his true self.

In the second half, "Racing in the Street" shifts the perspective to the man's point of view. He reminisces about his love for building and racing cars and the camaraderie he shared with his friends. But beneath the surface, he struggles with the burdens of adulthood and financial insecurity, feeling the weight of his choices on both himself and his partner. He longs to make her happy, but can he change who he is at his core?

As thinkers like Fromm and Plato suggest, love requires work, like fine-tuning a car. But how much sacrifice is necessary to sustain a relationship? Sometimes, despite genuine love, two people simply cannot make it work.

Klahr emphasizes that while the songs shape the narrative, they don't dictate it entirely:

> The script (the lyrics) is not the film. I'm also adding ideas to the imagery that aren't present in the lyrics—like the male character's struggles with employment in both "acts." Although neither song mentions this issue, I use it as a subtext, showing images of a government employment office. This becomes a motivation to change, especially for the boyfriend The Shangri-Las sing about, who "doesn't wear those dirty black boots anymore." My imagery suggests he's changing not because the singer has domesticated him, as the lyrics imply, but because he realizes he needs to transition into adulthood.[11]

A Thousand Julys (2010) is a two-act melodrama told through overlapping comic book pages. The story follows the tentative union of two older protagonists. In Act One, Astrud Gilberto's rendition of "Gentle Rain" plays in reverse, underscoring a haze of faces. Were these two once friends who shared a one-night stand? Or do they repeatedly encounter each other at social gatherings? Their reluctance hints at emotional baggage preventing them from diving into a relationship.

After a silent, out-of-focus interlude, the song returns in its original form, with the lines—"We both are lost and alone in the world / Walk me in the gentle rain"—evoking the loneliness that draws them together. Though their hesitation remains unexplained, the weight of past heartbreak lingers. Ultimately, they decide to take a chance on love, driving off together, suggesting that what began as a fleeting encounter may become something deeper.

The superimposed comic pages reflect the confusion and uncertainty that often accompanies new relationships. As the narrative progresses, the fragmented pages coalesce, mirroring the couple's emotional journey toward unity. By the end, they realize that even with the risks involved, love is preferable to solitude.

Amid *The Couplets* lies the *Nimbus Trilogy*: *Nimbus Smile* (2009), *Nimbus Seeds* (2009), and *Cumulonimbus* (2010). This trilogy follows a mysterious romantic triangle that unfolds across the films.

Nimbus Smile opens with a sense of unease. A man watches from a window, seemingly contemplating something sinister—perhaps even a leap to his death. The scene shifts to a woman at a party, conversing with another man. Subtle objects—a subway token, beds, sofas, nighttime walks—hint at infidelity. The man in the window reappears, and this time, he jumps. Was he her lover or husband? The Velvet Underground's "Pale Blue Eyes" plays as the woman grapples with divided affections.

Strangely, the woman in the film does not have blue eyes, raising questions about who the film is really about.

In *Nimbus Seeds*, Klahr reuses the same images but overlays them with natural sounds—brushing teeth, flushing toilets, wind chimes, drilling, footsteps. This juxtaposition creates tension, suggesting that affairs are mundane, part of life's everyday routine.

In the final film, *Cumulonimbus*, familiar sounds return, but this time we meet an older married couple. The man is revealed to be the Golden Age comic hero Flash, now alone after his wife's death. Struggling with grief and financial hardship, he withdraws into memories of her. Eventually, he encounters the woman from the earlier films, and despite their complicated pasts, they fall in love.

By the trilogy's end, it's clear that Flash and the woman have found love, but unresolved questions remain. Who was the man in the window? Was he her first lover? Did he take his own life, or is this a surreal time-travel story where Flash reconnects with his younger wife? Regardless, the trilogy beautifully portrays love's resilience—even in the face of loss and uncertainty.

Sugar Slim Says (2010), performed by Chocolate Genius Incorporated, takes a darker approach to love, exploring bitterness and resentment. A man lashes out at a former lover with venomous anger. Klahr's visuals shift from his usual romanticized collage style to gritty imagery—shots of toilets, seedy clubs, booze, cigarettes, dirty dishes, and unsavory characters—all reflecting the protagonist's disillusionment.

In the second part, the anger softens, replaced by fragile nostalgia. A gentler, unfiltered love emerges—still raw and painful, but real.

Wednesday Morning Two A.M. (2009) tells the story of a woman haunted by memories of lost love. The Shangri-Las' "I Never Learn" plays twice in the film, marking the protagonist's emotional arc. In the first half, she drifts between dream and memory, grappling with the sting of rejection.

The second half shifts to textured, colored backdrops, symbolizing her gradual descent into sleep. As her memories blur, the pain of heartbreak begins to ease. By the film's end, she appears on the cusp of moving on, having confronted her sorrow.

Kiss the Rain (2012) and *The Street of Everlasting Rain* (2012) together form the mini-series *The Rain Couplets*. Like *The Couplets* series, these films explore romantic love, but with a focus on the fading love of an older couple—the moment when one partner realizes they no longer love the other. In that instant, both of their worlds begin to unravel.

Although both films share overlapping imagery, the soundtracks distinguish them emotionally. *Kiss the Rain* features Audrey Hepburn's rendition of "Moon River" and Wes Montgomery's version of "It Was a Very Good Year." Meanwhile, *The Street of Everlasting Rain* is set to The Walker Brothers' "I Don't Want to Hear It Anymore" and Burt Bacharach's "A House is Not a Home." These shared visuals create continuity, but the differing musical scores lend each film a distinct emotional resonance.

Nimbus Seeds

Kiss the Rain uses a blend of sketches, illustrations, photos, and found materials to depict the excitement of new love alongside the slow dissolution of a long-term relationship. The narrative follows a man who leaves his marriage for a younger woman, enticed by the allure of new dreams and possibilities. However, as the story unfolds, the tone shifts. The jilted partner wanders their empty home, haunted by the absence of love. Simultaneously, the man—despite the initial thrill of his younger lover—begins to feel a creeping unease, suspecting he's made a profound mistake. He embodies the archetype philosophers have warned of: the man who trades in a perfectly good car for a shiny new one, only to realize that the problem was never the car. Beneath the surface, the story reflects on mortality—a fear of aging and the naïve hope that new love might somehow stave off death.

In *The Street of Everlasting Rain*, gossiping neighbors weave a chorus of judgmental whispers, speculating that the younger woman doesn't truly love the man and may be seeing someone else. These rumors begin to echo the man's own growing doubts. He finds himself trapped in a house that no longer feels like a home, empty of love and full of regret. Alternatively, the film can be seen as a nostalgic reflection on the life he once had—now irretrievably lost. As remorse sets in, he questions the impulsiveness of his choice. The film's final line, "Oh, please be there still in love with me," suggests that both the man and, perhaps, his ex-wife are struggling with the fallout of his departure.

As I've mentioned before, Klahr's approach to narrative often leaves gaps that invite viewers to interpret the story in their own way. *The Rain Couplets* are a great example of this. However, it turns out my interpretation wasn't entirely accurate, at least when compared to Klahr's original intent.

As discussed earlier, Klahr's narrative style often leaves intentional gaps, inviting viewers to interpret the story in their own way. *The Rain Couplets* exemplify this openness, though, as Klahr himself explains, my interpretation differs from his original intent:

> Interesting interpretation, I suppose, suggested by the number of elderly people shown living in the apartment—the "nosy neighbors" you referred to—and by the songs chosen: "A Very Good Year" and, in the second Couplet, "A House Is Not a Home." However, the woman is depicted as young, but so is the man, and the male singer is described as both a girl and a boy. So, I'm trying to depict a longer-term relationship for younger people—1–2 years—not a marriage, though the couple is living together. But I can see how the songs could skew the story and its protagonists toward middle age, a longer relationship, and possibly marriage—especially the Bacharach. This kind of loose continuity is classic "Klahrian" suggestiveness, no?[12]

In Klahr's version, the woman leaves the man, and he remains alone in his apartment, longing for her return—a return that is unlikely to happen.

Klahr elaborates on the use of overlapping imagery in *The Rain Couplets*:

> The repetition as variants, with small degrees of new information, creates a kind of novelistic effect. Process-wise, I received some negative feedback about the choice of "Moon River," so I felt I had to extend the piece to make it fuller, as I had done with *The Nimbus Trilogy* and the use of the Velvet Underground's "Pale Blue Eyes." Once I made the second Couplet, I was happy with how it expanded the story while repeating many of the same shots, which now read differently, being placed in a new montage sequence.
>
> I was also pleased with the tender vulnerability of the emotionally fragile singers—Audrey Hepburn with "Moon River" in the first Couplet, and Burt Bacharach with "A House Is Not a Home" in the second. This created a more subtle female/male viewpoint shift, though not as direct a juxtaposition as the songs in *April Snow*. Here, the shift is much more elusive, as is the storytelling, which is expanded by the repetition of variants with slight additions of new information, creating that novelistic effect.[13]

Klahr's most recent series, *The Blue Rose of Forgetfulness* (2021), delves deeply into love, desire, romance, and the complexities of difficult relationships. The blue rose—a nonexistent flower—has long symbolized something mysterious and unattainable, serving as a fitting metaphor for the elusive nature of love in this six-part series. Throughout the films, a persistent sense of restlessness, anxiety, and doubt permeates the atmosphere. Fragmented voices, fleeting faces, and subtle hints of deception, murder, adultery, and loss hang in the background.

At times, particularly in some films from *The Blue Rose of Forgetfulness* series, I find myself uncertain about what is happening—but that ambiguity is part of the experience. Klahr's films are often felt rather than fully understood. The opening film, *Monogram* (2019), is especially mystifying—more so than many of Klahr's already enigmatic works. This sense of mystery is precisely what gives his films their emotional resonance and timeless appeal. The narrative, loosely framed between spring and late summer, could be interpreted as following the sexual exploits of a shady door-to-door salesman. We encounter various objects: products, gift boxes, hotels, references to benzedrine, and street maps of neighborhoods. At one point, the salesman appears to be beaten up. There's arson, police involvement, and a woman running through the streets—or perhaps it is a cutout figure moving across the maps.

In *Swollen Kisses* (2019)—which recalls themes from *Elevator Music*—a seemingly desperate woman obsessively searches for her ideal man, or perhaps becomes consumed by the one she already has, who eventually abandons her. *Capitulations Promise* (2020), a hauntingly beautiful piece, features Lana Del Rey's hypnotic track "Honeymoon," underscoring the struggles of a troubled couple. Despite their difficulties, the couple seems determined to move forward, as suggested by the lyrics, "there's nothing to lose now that I've found you." Robert Mitchum appears in the film, though his role is ambiguous—perhaps the dangerous lover Lana sings about or a father figure

Capitulations Promise

Blue Sun

hoping she'll leave the man behind. In the end, all we know is that the woman confesses, "I lied" about another man. When Mitchum asks why, there is no answer—because, in matters of the heart, explanations are often elusive, and logic is seldom followed.

Blue Sun (2020) presents overlapping comic book pages from a compilation book of Agent X-9 daily newspaper comic strips (1967–1969), drawn by Al Williamson, filled with references to the FBI, spies, espionage, and characters including a blonde and a brunette. The layering of these elements evokes a sense of drifting through purgatory—a limbo between memory, fantasy, and reality. The film blurs the boundaries between these dimensions, creating a chaotic fusion of emotions, thoughts, and recollections.

It feels as though we are simultaneously experiencing multiple realities—both inner and outer—reflecting a truth familiar to all of us. We present a public persona, but beneath that surface lies a tangled web of unspoken truths, half-formed thoughts, and fleeting memories, not yet fully processed. The atmosphere is dense with tension and violence, hinting at crime, murder, and ominous figures lurking just out of sight. Yet the juxtaposition of bird calls and passing cars grounds the scene in everyday life. The final shot—a woman in a man's arms—leaves us with a fleeting hope that love and connection might be within reach.

The most powerful depiction of love and sacrifice in the series is *Alcestis* (2021), a modern retelling of the Greek myth. Alcestis' willingness to sacrifice her life for her husband, Admetus, represents the ultimate act of love.

However, in Klahr's interpretation, things go awry. After descending into the underworld, Alcestis has an intimate encounter with multiple lovers. Upon her return to the surface, she discovers that Admetus—ever the opportunist—has run off with another woman. Yet still, it's the thought that counts, right?

The series concludes with *The Blue Rose of Forgetfulness* (2020), which opens with the sound of ocean waves and leads into a cover of "Nature Boy" by Big Star. A heartbroken woman reflects on an encounter with a man she could never truly possess. Before parting, the man imparts a profound truth, *"The best we can do is to love and be loved in return."* Too often, we focus on receiving love rather than giving it, forgetting that one cannot exist without the other. And, when love does happen, it inevitably brings both joy and sorrow, for loss and pain are intrinsic to love.

Klahr's most recent film, *Interstitial Romance (Warm Novelette)* (2024), unfolds across two sides of a comic book page. The narrative is filled with serious conversations, embraces, and kisses—but are these romantic gestures or farewells? It remains unclear, which is precisely the point. Klahr's exploration of love, desire, and romance is deliberately ambiguous. His characters navigate emotions that are fluid and unpredictable, shifting without warning from one extreme to another.

Love is blindness. Love hurts. Love is a battlefield. Love, meant to be the sunrise of human existence—the river that quenches our thirst in the desert of loneliness—often reduces us to temperamental children on a playground, hurling hurt at one another.

Klahr's films capture the full spectrum of love's experience: the sensual and the cold, the deceit and the devotion, the loneliness, betrayal, fear, and regret. In his world, the line between love and grief is razor-thin, fraying when neglected. Frequently, his protagonists end up heartbroken and alone, yet they—and we—continue to return to love, hoping for a different outcome each time.

Klahr's characters embody Nietzsche's observation that when we are in love we often see things most decidedly as they are not. Erich Fromm's critique of love under capitalism also resonates throughout Klahr's films, where love is distorted by consumerist values. As Fromm argued, "the principle underlying capitalistic society and the principle of love are incompatible."[14] Klahr's characters experience love mediated by consumerism—defined by appearances, status, and material possessions.

In this framework, love becomes akin to window shopping or browsing online stores, always searching for the next best thing to enhance one's existence. Approaching love as a commodity inevitably leads to failure.

Perhaps the problem lies in our expectations. We demand too much from love—expecting it to be eternal, all-encompassing, and capable of solving all our problems. But maybe love's role is simpler, if no less significant. As

Robert Pollard sings in "Choking Tara," "Can't imagine that all our troubles will go away, but I could catch her and break the falls. I could snatch her with beaks and claws."[15]

Love can make things better—but it cannot make them perfect.

NOTES

1 Erich Fromm, *The Art of Loving*. New York: Harper Perennial Modern Classics, 2019, p. 1.
2 Fromm, *The Art of Loving*, p. 72.
3 Email exchange with the Author, August 2024.
4 Email exchange with the Author, August 2024.
5 Email exchange with the Author, August 2024.
6 Email exchange with the Author, August 2024.
7 Email exchange with the Author, August 2024.
8 Email exchange with the Author, August 2024.
9 Email exchange with the Author, August 2024.
10 Email exchange with the Author, August 2024.
11 Email exchange with the Author, August 2024.
12 Email exchange with the Author, September 2024.
13 Email exchange with the Author, September 2024.
14 Fromm, *The Art of Loving*, p. 121.
15 From the song, "Choking Tara", written by Robert Pollard, performed by Guided by Voices, 1997.

Do the Collapse

5

Consumerism, along with its patron saint, Capitalism, lingers uncomfortably throughout Klahr's films—and indeed, throughout all collage art. However, it would be reductive to link collage solely with capitalism, given its presence in communist countries, where it served both to support and critique government policies. For example, Russian artists employed collage to promote government initiatives and the latest films. Similarly, collage appeared in North American advertising and war propaganda, such as a 1941 ad featuring women alongside a giant carrot to promote refrigerators and a 1942 War Bonds poster showing two children wearing gas masks. In later decades, collage became a staple of television advertising, especially during the 1950s and 1960s.

Today, collage—particularly in animation—has become closely associated with American artists, perhaps reflecting the hyper-consumerism and capitalism of the culture that produces it. Yet, collage is inherently contradictory. While it often critiques or mocks the flood of commercial, pop culture, and mass media imagery, it depends on those same images for its existence. Without the consumer imagery it critiques, Klahr's work, as we know it, would not exist.

Unlike the more blunt critiques of consumerism and capitalism found in the collage animation of Stan Vanderbeek, Martha Colburn, and even Terry Gilliam (though Gilliam's work often feels like an unfocused tantrum against everything proper and powerful), Klahr adopts a more nuanced, self-aware approach. He acknowledges his own position as a consumer within the system he critiques:

> I view critique as important, but as just one of many perspectives my collage work addresses. Generally, I find work that prioritizes critique to be didactic and less interesting than work in which critique is integrated as one artistic perspective among many. *The Pettifogger* is a clear representation of how I position myself in terms of a critique of capitalism. The film uses larceny and conning as metaphors for unfettered, virulent capitalism.

DOI: 10.1201/9781003427223-5

> However, *The Pettifogger*'s emphasis on experimental film form might obscure this for many more politically minded viewers. Its formal complexity certainly doesn't offer a populist engagement that is readily understandable to those not deeply immersed in experimental narrative aesthetics.[1]

Indeed, Klahr's films—*The Pharaoh's Belt, Altair, Govinda*, *Downs Are Feminine,* and the aforementioned *The Pettifogger*—each convey, in different ways, the failed promises of the so-called American Dream, revealing a world dominated by the phoniness and limitations of consumerism.

Some of Klahr's most direct critiques of capitalism and consumerism emerge in *Antigenic Drift* (2007) and the series *Circumstantial Pleasures* (2016–2019). Described by Klahr as "a punch in the nose for the viewer from its first film," these works adopt harsher tones and materials. The lush, nostalgic imagery of the mid-20th century gives way to junkier, more contemporary elements.

Klahr's shift toward modern materials began in the early 2000s:

> I began collecting plastics, mostly packaging, as a significant signpost of the contemporary world. I had also asked myself a simple question, comparing my knowledge of the world I had grown up in to the present, and wondered if I could describe the latter as clearly. I found I couldn't, so I started to focus on the contemporary as a subject.[2]

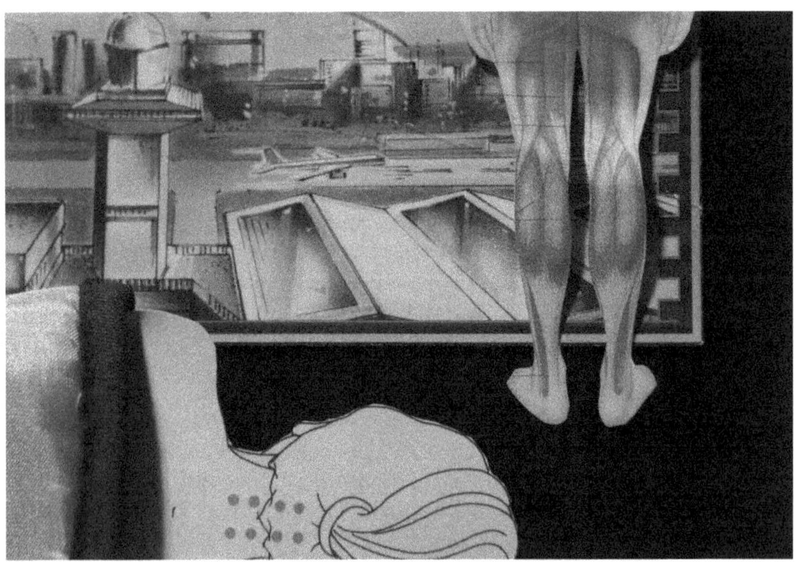

Antigenic Drift

Antigenic Drift—Klahr's first digital film—marks a distinct departure from his earlier work. The nostalgic allure of the past is replaced by a stark focus on the horrors of the present, particularly the cold, inhuman, and wasteful nature of capitalism. Gone are the charming images of the 1950s, replaced by consumer debris—plastics, tickets, and illness. Made years before the COVID-19 pandemic, the film is eerily prescient.

This world is devoid of humans. We hear only the voices of airline attendants and the murmurs of airport passengers. Skeletal figures and faceless cutouts populate the scenes—a stark reflection of a society dominated by "stuff," where humans are reduced to mere vacuums, consuming endlessly. *Antigenic Drift* is haunting, unlike anything Klahr had previously created.

The film's origins trace back to an article Klahr read in *The New Yorker* about pandemics:

> This article described 'antigenic drift,' which is the name scientists have given to the process by which viruses replicate themselves and mutate to stay viable in partially immune populations. I was attracted to this idea, not only for what it said about pandemics but also for how it related to collage—source materials migrating from their original contexts and recontextualizing themselves into fresh contexts, while still retaining part of their original history.[3]

"Is anything wrong?" a voice asks during *Circumstantial Pleasures*.

The answer is yes—a whole lot is wrong.

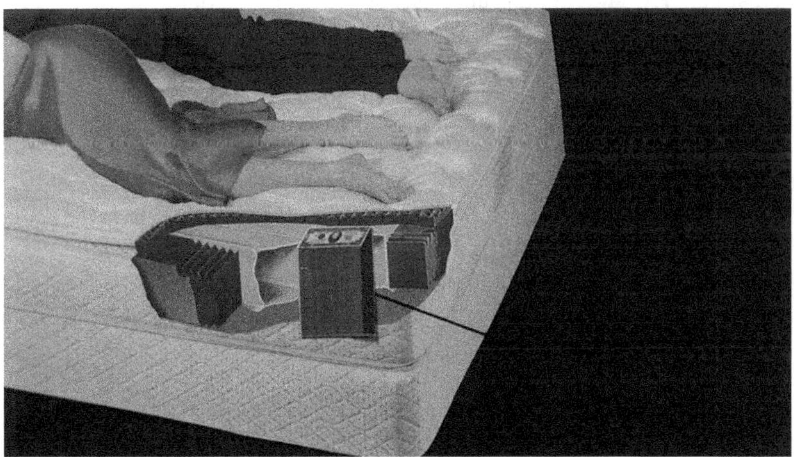

Circumstantial Pleasures

In today's world, we are bombarded by conflicting and outrageous claims, leading to widespread cynicism. As Hannah Arendt warned in a 1974 interview,

> A people that can no longer believe anything cannot make up its mind. It is deprived not only of its capacity to act but also of its capacity to think and to judge. And with such a people, you can then do what you please.[4]

This is the chaotic world Klahr explores in *Circumstantial Pleasures*, a series of six short films that critique capitalism's destructive effects on humanity and the planet. Featuring music by David Rosenboom, Tom Recchion, and the haunting wail of Scott Walker, the films juxtapose world leaders, politicians, dictators, and assassins with familiar capitalist symbols—cars, highways, oil barrels, and currency. A recurring image of a headless Statue of Liberty underscores the series' grim message.

The series originated in 2013 when Klahr first created a film titled *Circumstantial Pleasures.* Dissatisfied with the result, he re-edited it and retitled it *Serrated Edge.* Yet, even that second version felt incomplete.

> I realized that there wasn't just one film to create with all the contemporary imagery I had collected, but a whole series which I would title *Circumstantial Pleasures.*[5]

During this period, Klahr struggled with narcolepsy and the side effects of medication, which he believes amplified the fear and rage permeating his work.

The opening film, *Capitalist Roadsters* (2016), transports viewers into a distinctively darker Klahr universe, one reminiscent of the ominous sci-fi films of the 1970s. It depicts a world of menace and waste—smog, pollution, Trump, currency, consumer packaging, oil barrels, factories, cardboard, shipping containers, traffic, and bundles of cash. This landscape is nearly devoid of humans, dominated instead by currency and material objects.

Unlike Klahr's earlier work, which often draws on the lush, vintage imagery of the mid-20th century, *Capitalist Roadsters* immerses us in an ugly world of unsightly cheapness—a post-apocalyptic setting bereft of life. The absence of human presence contributes to an unsettling atmosphere of anxiety, tension, and alienation, reflecting a society weighed down by the relentless accumulation of junk, the discarded byproducts of capitalism. As Chris Stults aptly notes, *Capitalist Roadsters* is "a parade of images about the nihilism of capitalism."

In *Ramification Lesions (Microbial Stress)* (2019), Klahr delves even deeper into contemporary anxieties. The film weaves together repeated images of the gallery shooter who assassinated the Russian ambassador to

Turkey in 2016 and depictions of figures, such as Putin, Kim Jung Un, Hillary Clinton, Trump, Jeff Bezos, and Mark Zuckerberg. These political and economic figures are juxtaposed with assorted packaging material and plastic, reinforcing the sense of a chaotic, cluttered world.

The film resembles a relentless newsfeed, blending headlines with consumer detritus, environmental crises, weapons, hostages, and mass murderers. Klahr presents a disturbing fusion of politics, economics, and environmental disasters, interspersed with scenes of protests and a striking image of a headless Statue of Liberty—a grim symbol of a world in disarray. This is a depiction of reality in chaotic freefall.

In *Ratchet the Margin* (2016), Klahr shifts focus to the pharmaceutical industry, using surreal imagery to convey the ways in which individuals are trapped within systems of consumption and control. The film unfolds in an eerie, fragmented space, moving between an emergency room, abstract shapes and textures, a door, and a mattress. A man lies trapped, with a pill ominously placed nearby—capturing the sense of people as prisoners to the pharmaceutical industry.

Throughout the film, electricity towers loom in the background, alongside fast food and subtle, sinister elements lurking just beneath the surface. This imagery raises unsettling questions: What exactly are we consuming? What's hidden in the food? The drugs? The film provokes viewers to confront the troubling reality that we know so little about the products we rely on—and that these very products may be complicit in our entrapment.

Virulent Capital

In *Virulent Capital* (2018), a sci-fi-inspired film, capitalism is fittingly portrayed as a virus. We are all infected, sickened by consumerism and its endless, hollow promises of wholeness, perfection, and satisfaction. The film critiques how consumerism encourages us to seek meaning and identity through material possessions rather than introspection. It adopts an anti-narrative, anti-audience stance, focusing on junk—the detritus of consumerism that fills our lives with things we don't truly need.

Accompanied by an eerie electronic noise soundtrack—evocative of the unsettling hum of a factory—the film provokes a visceral sense of anger. However, this anger is not directed at the *Throbbing Gristle*-like score but at the grim truth, it exposes: we, as individuals, are insignificant compared to the endless flow of packaging and "stuff" that consumerism delivers to us. In this system, the value of human life is eclipsed by the value placed on material goods.

Klahr's shift toward this harsher, more confrontational direction feels inevitable. Over time, he came to recognize that the consumer promises of his youth were deceptive, destined to collapse under the weight of their own fraudulence. We were conned, with the American Dream functioning as a kind of pettifogger—a legalistic deceiver. And when we inevitably awaken to the reality that this dream is a nightmare, the system offers its solution: numbing us into passive submission. This, they hope, will make the unbearable tolerable.

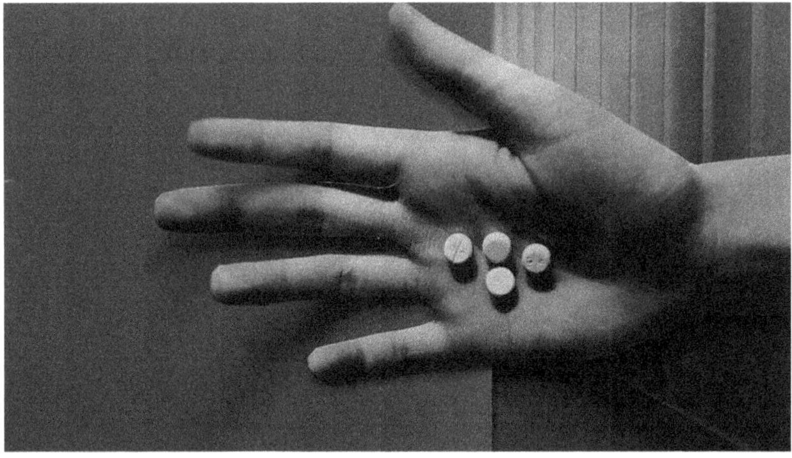

Circumstantial Pleasures

High Rise (2016) stands out as an anomaly within Klahr's body of work. Filmed on a phone camera from a high-speed train in China, it presents an unrelenting portrait of endless apartment buildings—towering, phallic structures stripped of meaning. Sparse patches of greenery briefly interrupt the monotony, only to emphasize the desolate, lifeless nature of the landscape. The absence of human presence heightens the unsettling atmosphere, offering a bleak, depopulated vision of urban sprawl.

The final film, *Circumstantial Pleasures* (2019), opens with the unsettling image of a seemingly lifeless woman, accompanied by an ominous, bald creature. As the film unfolds, fragmented imagery follows: body parts marked with red spots, a toilet, oil bins, wheelchairs, needles, currency, pills, and pollution. A chest with a surgical scar hints at the violent intrusion of consumerism into the human body. In this world, bodies and objects merge—humanity fuses with the junk it consumes. Cybernetic forms emerge, representing the transformation of people into hybrids shaped by the detritus of modern consumption.

American currency recurs throughout the film, emphasizing the central message: everything revolves around money—at all costs. Humans are rendered as mere afterthoughts in this ruthless system. Klahr drives home the idea that, in the grand scheme of capitalism, human life holds little value compared to the relentless pursuit of profit.

Enhancing the film's disquieting tone is Scott Walker's harrowing, angry, and utterly bizarre 21-minute song/rant, *SDSS1416+13B (Zercon, a Flagpole Sitter).* Walker's unsettling composition reinforces the visual horror of *Circumstantial Pleasures*, amplifying the film's themes of alienation and the dehumanizing impact of unchecked consumerism.

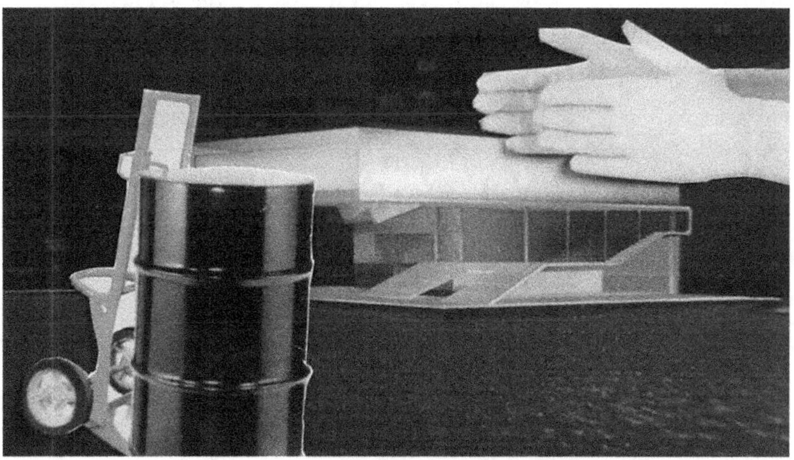

Circumstantial Pleasures

There are no readily available solutions in *Antigenic Drift* or the *Circumstantial Pleasures* series. Klahr seems to be grappling with the chaos himself, perhaps hoping that viewers leave the theatre—or wherever films are watched these days—feeling horrified, nauseous, and angry.

The harsh, unsettling tone of these films caught many programmers off guard. As a result, the films were rarely screened—at least not until 2020, when the unwelcome arrival of the COVID-19 pandemic shifted perceptions.

In a May 2020 interview with Courtney Stephens, Klahr reflected:

"*Circumstantial Pleasures* got nothing but rejections because the urgency of what it so abrasively describes makes for a challenging experience."[6] Once COVID hit, "the harshness was no longer off-putting."[7]

After a February 2020 screening, filmmaker Ken Jacobs even told Klahr, "Your film is right on time!"[8]

Klahr, much like the virus itself, viewed international supply chains as largely invisible—until crises revealed their fragility. In the same interview, he elaborated:

> I keep seeing the way the pandemic foregrounds the absurdity and limitations of money as an agreed-upon social fiction. Far too many people in power in the United States, especially on the right, treat capitalism like it's a self-correcting, natural system. But then a problem like this arises and capitalism doesn't react, because it doesn't have empathy; people do. Capitalism has no motive besides profit. It can't and won't acquire a conscience until people forcefully demand that it does.[9]

This phase of Klahr's oeuvre is, in a challenging yet thought-provoking way, both taxing and exhausting to digest, especially for the way it abandons the narrative. The films hover on the edge of horror, evoking a lingering sense of dread and anxiety—much like watching a horror movie, except that this nightmare increasingly reflects our reality.

NOTES

1 Email with the Author, October 2024.
2 Email with the Author, October 2024.
3 https://bombmagazine.org/articles/2020/05/27/lewis-klahr/
4 https://www.transcend.org/tms/2017/02/hannah-arendt-from-an-interview/
5 Email with the Author, October 2024.
6 https://bombmagazine.org/articles/2020/05/27/lewis-klahr/
7 https://bombmagazine.org/articles/2020/05/27/lewis-klahr/.
8 https://bombmagazine.org/articles/2020/05/27/lewis-klahr/.
9 https://bombmagazine.org/articles/2020/05/27/lewis-klahr/.

Big Time Wrestling

6

> What causes us to suffer is not in the past or the future: it is here, now, in our memory, in our expectations. we long for timelessness, we endure the passing of time: we suffer time. Time is suffering.[1]

Clocks, shattered watches, calendars, childhood memories, aging protagonists, youth serums, skeletal figures, and other markers of time appear frequently throughout Lewis Klahr's work, creating a disorienting blend of nostalgia and melancholy. Time is a central theme in Klahr's art; he often describes his work as exploring "the pastness of the present." Like a pop culture archaeologist, Klahr unearths ephemera—print advertisements, comic books, film footage, magazine and book illustrations, pop songs, and various 3D objects—from the past. However, this is not mere nostalgia. Klahr reanimates these forgotten artifacts, breathing new life and meaning into mementos that once held cultural and economic significance.

The Pettifogger

DOI: 10.1201/9781003427223-6

"Most of my art," Klahr explains, "details the experience of then and now—lived time—that sense of the gap in time between what once was and what is, that gives nostalgia its uncanny, stomach-churning power."[2]

This sense of the "pastness of the present" in Klahr's work creates a collision of past and present imagery, producing a temporal discomfort—a sense that we are never quite sure when we are. It is as though we move through dreams, memories, and history all at once, wobbling between timelines. Time is often simplified into three segments: past, present, and future. Yet, as Saint Augustine argued, the only thing that truly exists is the present. The past is gone, and the future has not yet arrived. According to him, past and future are mental constructs, created to help us make sense of our experiences.

In *The Order of Time*, Carlo Rovelli builds on this idea, suggesting that the present itself is an illusion:

> There is our past: all the events that happened before what we can witness now. There is our future: the events that will happen after the moment from which we can see the here and now. Between this past and this future there is an interval that is neither past nor future and still has a duration.[3]

For Rovelli, a clear present or "now" cannot exist because no two moments are identical. What I write now will be read in the future, and each reader will interpret it differently, in their unique present. Rovelli concludes, "A common present does not exist."[4]

Jorge Luis Borges, in his essay *A New Refutation of Time*, similarly described time as "a succession of indivisible moments" and "a tireless labyrinth, a chaos, a dream."[5] He rejected the notion of one singular time, where everything is linked in a chain.

Saint Augustine identified "three tenses within time:

> The present of past things is memory, the present of present things is attention, and the present of future things is expectation."[6]

For Augustine, time exists only in the mind:

> It is in you, I say, that I measure time. As things pass by, they leave an impression in you; this impression remains after the things have gone into the past, and it is this impression which I measure in the present, not the things which, in their passage, caused the impression. It is this impression that I measure when I measure time. Therefore, either this itself is time or else I do not measure time at all.[7]

In other words, the present is a deeply personal, internal experience. Every thought, feeling, or action is shaped by echoes of the past. Each of us is a collection of the books we've read, the songs we've heard, the friends we've made, and the lovers we've embraced. We are ongoing manuscripts, continuously being written until the moment we stop. Even then, our traces live on in those we've touched—family, friends, lovers, and even enemies.

Klahr refers to his work as a "cultural autobiography." His films reflect both his personal life and the era in which he lived. Every element in his art—from parents and lovers to pop culture and filmmakers—represents aspects of his own experience. In unearthing these fragments, Klahr reconstructs the past and present through his subjective lens. There is no universal, external reality in his work; time, as Rovelli notes, "is shaped by our internal sense, that is to say, by our ordering of internal states within ourselves."[8]

Augustine likened this idea to poetry, where each stanza forms a part of the whole:

> The same thing happens in the entirety of a person's life, of which all his actions are parts; and the same thing happens in the entire sweep of human history, the parts of which are individual human lives.[9]

Klahr's films mirror Augustine's notion of life as poetry. He fuses materials, memories, and imaginings from mid-20th-century America, blending public and personal histories into something uniquely his own. As viewers, we also bring our own experiences into Klahr's films, projecting our narratives and emotions onto his work. This creates a fluid experience—our interpretation of his films today may differ from how we experienced them years ago.

Klahr's art explores time on multiple levels:

Collage Materials: His use of found objects and ephemera—forgotten relics from cultural history—serves as a tactile link to the past.

Passage of Time: Themes of aging, childhood, and mortality emerge in works like *False Aging*, the *Daylight Moon* quartet, *The Pharaoh's Belt*, *Helen of T*, *Lethe*, and *Pony Glass*.

Narrative Structure: His narrative approach often involves compressed or fragmented time, as seen in *1966*, *The Pettifogger*, *Saturn's Diary*, and the *Two Minutes to Zero* trilogy.

Klahr's films are mosaics of time—overlapping memories, pop culture fragments, and personal reflections. His narratives, like time itself, are elusive and multifaceted, inviting viewers to discover their own meanings within his carefully constructed chaos. Through his unique lens, Klahr reveals that time is not merely something we measure—it is something we live, feel, and continuously reconstruct.

The Pettifogger

COLLAGE MATERIALS

The use of collage materials is inherently rooted in the past—these elements must, by necessity, already exist—and often evokes a sense of childhood. Collage is not just a child's introduction to art; the materials themselves carry an intrinsic nostalgia. It feels as if the collage artist is reaching back into the past, drawing on memories of shapes, colors, textures, and sounds. In Klahr's work, there's a sense of a grown-up child still playing with his toys. His use of materials from his childhood extends that period of innocence, wonder, and imagination—a time without boundaries, full of infinite possibilities, and, above all, a world a child could control.

During my own childhood in the 1970s and 1980s, I spent hours immersed in hockey cards, creating scrapbooks filled with pictures and statistics, playing table hockey games, and embarking on imaginative adventures with friends. We reenacted *The Hardy Boys* mysteries or *Star Wars* storylines outdoors. I even invented my own hockey games using trading cards, and building entire matches. When the cards weren't enough, I created a full National Hockey League schedule for my beloved Montreal Canadiens, mirroring the real one, and used dice to determine the outcomes. These activities gave me a sense of control—although always with a hint of unpredictability, as I had to abide by the roll of the dice. I recorded radio broadcasts to replay the Canadiens' goals, reliving those fleeting moments of joy over and over again. It wasn't just about happiness—it was a way to capture and hold onto time, to preserve those moments before they slipped away.

As I grew older, my focus shifted to popular music. Like many of my generation, I started making mixtapes, seizing control over the music—no longer dependent on radio stations, DJs, or record labels. Creating my own order and mood through mixtapes gave me a sense of safety in what felt like an unpredictable reality. While I didn't fully grasp the concept of mortality back then, these acts of creation offered some comfort from the uncertainties of life.

Klahr acknowledges that some of his work involved "avoidance of the realities of aging,"[10] particularly in his early collage films:

> My interest in collage wouldn't have been sustainable all these decades, if it wasn't an interrogation of what the mystery of time passing is and by extension what that might mean about the mystery of life and death. I find the difference between now and then to be the most uncanny experience I've ever had. There's control and power via the miniaturization and living of other lives different than my own through my creation of fictive worlds and timelines. There's escape too. but I've experienced a change in my relation to my collected found materials.[11]

In earlier works like *1966*, Klahr's use of collage leaned toward nostalgic preservation. However, by the time he made *Sixty-Six*, his relationship with the materials had evolved:

> It's become more a way of communicating, a preferred mytho-poetic language to use to interrogate and convey my experiences of lived time and memory, than trying to hold onto specific objects encoded in my memory. I mean what am I really attached to in these mid-20th century discards? Mostly a color and textural sense that remains a primary attraction for me and source of sensual pleasure.[12]

As discussed in earlier chapters, Klahr often explores memory from a child's perspective. This theme is central to the series *Picture Books for Adults* and the mini-feature film *The Pharaoh's Belt.* The *Daylight Moon* quartet also captures the shift from childhood innocence to a growing awareness of the world's complexities.

In *Valise* (2004), Klahr weaves together found archival audio about gods with striking illustrations of stars, guiding viewers on a journey toward

Valise

new lands and cultural discovery. Iconic images like a zeppelin, a deep-sea diver, and an old baseball broadcast evoke fragments of Klahr's memories. Listening to baseball while daydreaming stirs nostalgia, while the deep-sea diver might symbolize the young Klahr exploring a mysterious world, shadowed by the enigmatic presence of adulthood.

This blend of baseball, astronomy, chess, nature, classrooms, and small-town life—depicted through vibrant illustrations—reflects a child's idealized imagination. The magic of Klahr's work lies in its ability to invite the audience to fill the spaces with their own memories. It evokes my childhood recollections of half-listening to Montreal Expos radio broadcasts while reading comic books or playing with sports cards.

The film concludes with Tobin Sprout's melancholic song, "Gas Daddy Gas," perhaps representing a longing for the blurred boundary between memory and reality. The song humanizes a father figure, embodying both mystery and a godlike presence.

Hard Green (2004) opens with war-themed comic book images, barely decipherable, set to scratchy bird songs and snippets of old radio broadcasts.

This collision of memory and nostalgia—pop culture alongside nature—captures the mind of a young boy. It hints at the contradictions between an idyllic childhood and the distant, violent realities of war.

Soft Ticket (2004) begins with birdsong on a scratchy record, accompanied by blurred images of a face that slowly shifts into scenes of baseball players—the gods of youth. The sounds of diners and ambient chatter reflect the fragmented thoughts of a child whose mind is filled with overlapping experiences: baseball cards, nature, diner conversations, and birdsong. Klahr captures this beautifully, with the camera scanning blurred images through a glass lens, evoking the fragmented, sensory past of a child.

The quartet concludes with *Daylight Moon* (2002), where scratchy record loops accompany images of planets, cars, motel rooms, an empty vault, a police officer, and various textures. A young girl's voice emerges from the record, expressing the innocence of youth alongside the confusing realities of life—or perhaps a romanticized vision of adulthood that a child cannot yet comprehend.

In Chapter 2, we hear eerie sounds from Charles Laughton's film *The Night of the Hunter.* Dreamy images, numbers, and objects appear amid more textures, reflecting the gradual loss of Klahr's childhood innocence. "It's a hard world for little creatures," a voice from the record warns.

Nick Drake's "River Man" accompanies the melancholic journey toward self-awareness, reflecting on the inevitability of change. The song conjures images of gray, rainy days and fleeting memories—moments that "come and go."

The *Daylight Moon* quartet is a paradox, creating a past that is both longed for and fictional. As explored earlier, the quartet represents a construction of distorted childhood memories shaped by pop culture and mass media. It forms a nostalgic ideal that exists only at the intersection of Klahr's personal experiences and the projections of his present self—memories shaped and reinterpreted through time.

FAST FORWARDING THROUGH TIME

> *"How long is forever?" asks Alice.*
> *"Sometimes just one second," replies the White* Rabbit.[13]

In *1966*, *The Pettifogger* (2011), and *Saturn's Diary*, Klahr structures the narratives around calendars or diaries. *1966* presents a school year through the eyes of a ten-year-old, while *Saturn's Diary* reflects a tedious period in

Saturn's Diary

the life of the god Saturn. More ambitiously, *The Pettifogger* compresses a year in the life of a conman into 60 minutes. It can even be argued that Klahr himself plays the role of a conman, appropriating all his materials from other sources.

Klahr's interest in compressed narrative draws inspiration from Robert Graves' writings on Greek myths. As Klahr explains:

> This kind of compression is an apt description of how cultures and individuals experience life on a daily basis. It's a process of summarization, where a greater understanding of events is stored by preserving key, essential aspects that can be reactivated with brief cues.[14]

The Pettifogger opens fittingly with an empty soap dish, signaling a world rooted in the mundane. The film continues with a sequence of fragmented images: an empty envelope, with geese passing by. It's 1963. The protagonist drifts through a routine of sex, drinking, hotels, gambling, card games, and fortune cookies. He's $434.34 in debt, desperate for a big break. At one point, he tells a woman, "I rehearsed telling you my life story." This line reflects a core theme: we fabricate ourselves, creating the stories of our lives through performance and illusion.

The protagonist is both a *flâneur* and a *flambeur*—a wanderer and a gambler—but his life steadily grows bleaker. The pace of the film slows, black spaces fill the screen, and the sounds of rain and thunder dominate. The man becomes increasingly isolated, lost in a haze of desperation. At one point, he appears in a hospital, unable to recall his identity. Why would he?

He's told so many origin stories and assumed so many identities that he's lost any sense of who he truly is.

The film ends with a melancholic shot of a Christmas tree ornament. Yet, after the credits roll, Klahr offers a flicker of hope: the image of a ceiling light. It's a small gesture, but it hints that perhaps the man might find his way out of his tangled mess.

Klahr admits that *The Pettifogger* is not an easy film to follow:

> Most viewers are extremely challenged by or unable to follow what happens to the Pettifogger as the film progresses. In this elliptical narrative, time compression has not only a psychological value but a metaphoric formal value as well.[15]

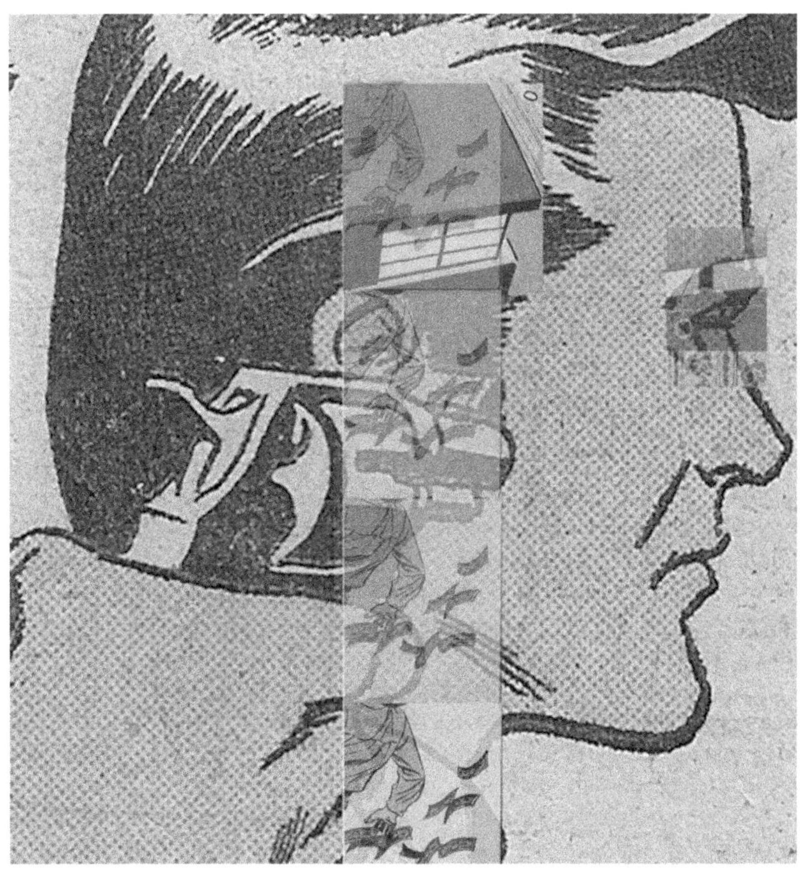

Two Minutes to Zero

In the *Two Minutes to Zero* trilogy, Lewis Klahr explores the visualization of memory and the past. Under a static camera, Klahr manually moves the pages of a crime comic book beneath the lens. The first film, *Two Days to Zero* (2004), spans 22 minutes. The second film, *Two Hours to Zero* (2004), lasts 8½ minutes, and the final film, *Two Seconds to Zero* (2003), runs just over a minute. Klahr explains:

> The overall progression aims to get the audience to memorize the imagery of the bank robber story well enough that when the final film plays, you can still follow the narrative even though it's been compressed to only one minute.[16]

Hints of a plot emerge: femme fatales, car chases, guns, surveillance, bound captives, and police appear—but it's nearly impossible to piece together a coherent storyline. The images blur, overlap, and disappear as quickly as they appear. But that's the point. Watching the trilogy feels like reading a comic book through the distracted mind of a child—someone more captivated by fragments of the images than by the narrative itself. The films oscillate between internal and external thoughts, and the use of song lyrics referring to dreams enhances the surreal quality. It's like watching someone's dream: familiar elements float in and out, but by the end, you're not entirely sure what just happened.

Throughout the trilogy, a mounting sense of urgency builds. However, the tension is not driven by the plot but by the relentless march of time. You want to grasp the moment, slow it down, and absorb it fully, but time refuses to comply. As someone once sang, "Time waits for no one."

Klahr brings motion to what is typically static, making his films feel like animated frames of mini paintings. It's as if we are caught between the physical act of reading a comic and the mental process of interpreting it—a blend of external observation and internal reflection.

The difficulty of following the comic book narrative shifts our focus toward the film's formal qualities. The fragmented images evoke the sensibilities of pop art, reminiscent of a Roy Lichtenstein painting. Klahr's films reflect the nature of memory and the past: no matter how hard we try, we can never fully capture them, leaving us with only unresolved fragments.

The trilogy's images evolve not through chronological time but according to their own rhythms. Time becomes elastic. Just as dreams can feel like they last for hours but span only minutes, Klahr's films explore the way time expands and contracts in unpredictable ways.

In a description that could easily apply to *Two Minutes to Zero*, Carlos Rovetti writes in *The Order of Time*, "There is no single time; there is a different duration for every trajectory, and time passes at different rhythms according to place and according to speed."[17]

TIME DECAY

Throughout Klahr's work, a pervasive sense of melancholy serves as a reminder that time is running out for all of us. This awareness has followed him since childhood but was heightened by the trauma of a car accident when he was 20 that left a lasting imprint on his personal life and artistic practice. Klahr reflects:

> I was backward-looking earlier than most people are. And certainly, my existential crisis in my second year of collage —when a friend and I were hit by a car as pedestrians, leading to my friend's death—profoundly triggered my awareness of my own mortality. It made me realize how much I wanted to be alive, something I wasn't sure of during my existential crisis.[18]

Klahr's attraction to collage extends beyond nostalgia and childhood play; it carries deeper whispers of mortality. As he explains:

> The mid-20th-century collage images I use most frequently are, in themselves, dead—dead by being outmoded. In one sense, I am bringing them back to life, which parallels my experience after the accident, when I found film and my purpose—a kind of rebirth. After the accident, in the hospital emergency room, I awakened lying on the gurney, with no concern for or knowledge of who or where I was, or how I got there. For a long moment, I was just pure consciousness, perceiving in the moment.
>
> Then the nurse noticed I was awake and asked me, 'Do you know who you are?' (standard concussion protocol). For a long moment, I didn't. When my memory finally kicked back in, I found the question funny. But when she asked a second time, I understood she was serious, and I answered.[19]

False Aging (2008) is one of Klahr's most profound meditations on the passage of time and the decay of the body. Dedicated to his late friend, filmmaker Mark Lapore, the film unfolds in three distinct sections.

The first section, possibly representing spring, youth, and hope, evokes a sense of optimism. The soundtrack, borrowed from *Valley of the Dolls*, reinforces this mood, suggesting life's possibilities. Yet even within this hopeful period, there are references to loneliness—the exhilaration of striving upward, only to be met with isolation.

In the second section, likely set in summer, Jefferson Airplane's "Lather" takes center stage. The narrative follows a man named Lather—a reference to shaving foam, symbolizing the transition into adulthood—who has reached his 30s. Despite his age, Lather clings to a youthful mindset, resisting the inevitability of growing older. The song's poignant line, "Is it true that I'm no longer young?" encapsulates his inner struggle, highlighting the tension between his sense of identity and the relentless passage of time. It emphasizes

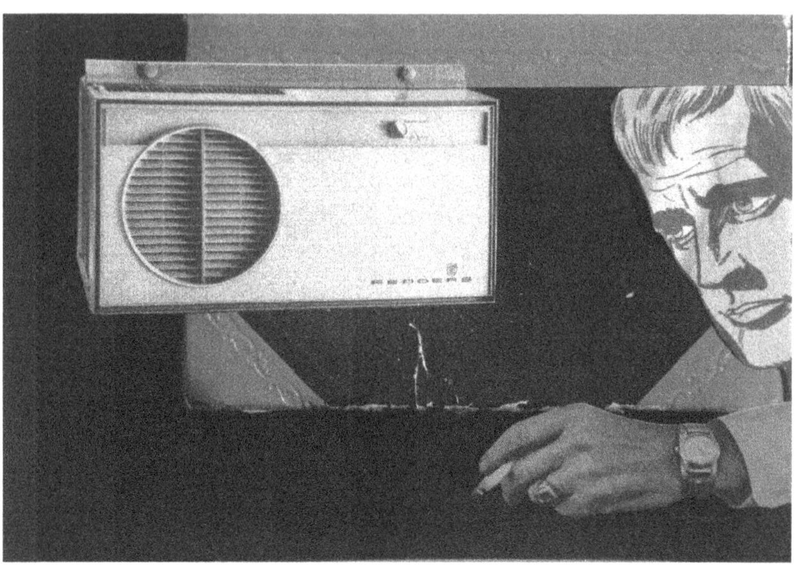

False Aging

the painful realization that the world he once knew has moved on without him, leaving him grappling with the irreversible loss of youth.

The final segment features Lou Reed and John Cale's "A Dream," written from the imagined perspective of their late mentor, Andy Warhol. The song reflects the arrival of old age. Reed and Cale, both in their 50s at the time, reference fall and snow—symbols of the passing seasons and the end of life's journey. The imagery in this section depicts an older man (portrayed through comic book drawings of David McCallum from *The Man from U.N.C.L.E.*), accompanied by cigarettes and a parked car, creating a somber, reflective atmosphere. Regrets, feuds, and aging dominate, as the speaker, Cale performing as Warhol, recounts a dream that feels like a meditation on a past long gone.

Klahr continuously reminds us of the passage of time through recurring motifs: a globe circles a mirror or door, library due date cards appear, and a clock ticks away. A yellow bird flutters throughout the film, symbolizing the illusion of freedom—a reminder that we are all prisoners of time.

As curator Mark McElhatten eloquently observed in 2008:

> Time is untruthful and mirrors prick the eye. Timelessness weighs lightly, duration is hard to endure. Still the living are younger than the dead. The departed seem to speak from a calm remove with an elephant's memory, more irksome and with greater feeling than we can command. Sometimes

> they miss being lost in these limited moments with us, smoking a cigarette, touching the earth, being short changed and anxious. Being. Fretting on the stage. It is then their remnants, their daily trivia and their questions haunt the air like a September song. And because we are breathing still, we think it is our breath and our song, and because we are breathing, it is.[20]

In *5 Days Till Tomorrow* (2022), a sense of impending doom permeates the narrative. The title evokes the tone of classic Hollywood sci-fi films, such as *20 Million Miles to Earth* and *The Day the Earth Stood Still.* Handless clocks, recurring throughout the film, enhance its eerie atmosphere.

Sparse piano notes echo through empty corridors, while skeletal figures and suffering characters populate a barren landscape. People clutch their foreheads in pain, seemingly afflicted by some environmental menace or pandemic. Haunting absences dominate the scenes. Has something terrible already occurred, or is it still to come?

The film features a bald woman, an empty bottle that may have once contained a virus, and the superhero Hourman lying on a sofa, affected like everyone else. Humans and superheroes alike are vulnerable, suggesting that no one is exempt from the ravages of time or illness.

Hourman, nicknamed "Tick Tock" for his punctuality, serves as both a nod to Klahr's comic book youth and a commentary on humanity's desire for invincibility. As a young scientist, Hourman invented Miraclo, a substance granting him superpowers for just one hour. In *5 Days Till Tomorrow*, the high cost of such desires becomes evident, mirroring the toll of the pandemic.

A man with a distorted, part-beast face reflects deeper themes of transformation and decay. Everyone in this world is disconnected, unwilling, or unable to speak, as the sense of an impending end looms. There are no saviors here—perhaps there never were.

Three Friends of the Cold Season (2024), completed as this book was being finalized, explores isolation, aging, death, and American mythology. Featuring songs by Dick Connette from the American folk project *Lost Forever*, the film is divided into three sections: a sailor, based on the legend of Alexander Selkirk, is stranded on an island, forced to accept that he will remain there for the rest of his life; an outlaw (Lazarus) senses his time is running out and prefers death to imprisonment; a man who abandoned his past life in youth now dreams of returning to a home frozen in time, untouched by aging. Yet he remains alone, confronting the irreversible consequences of his youthful decisions.

Each section is imbued with melancholy, loss, alienation, and the inescapable presence of death, underscoring the rapid passage of time. The film serves as a stark reminder: no matter the choices we make, we come into this world alone—and leave the same way.

Klahr has long been reluctant to discuss the car accident's impact on his films:

> It was too personally sacred, but I now see that was a bit of a mistake. People think I'm superficially nostalgic or sentimental, when in fact, I'm grappling with the experience of my life nearly ending at a very young age, before I had accomplished anything as an artist. Without knowing this part of my history, they don't understand that all those dedications at the end of my films come from a deep sense of gratitude for still being alive.[21]

Klahr's imagery reflects the nature of memory—fragmented and fleeting. These images emerge briefly before fading, much like the hazy moments between waking and sleeping. What remains are only traces, impressions of memory, and, ultimately, of time itself.

NOTES

1 Carlo Rovelli, *The Order of Time*. New York: Riverhead Books, 2018, p. 189.
2 Mark Wordsworth, *Bee Thousand*. New York: Continuum Press, 2011, p. 38.
3 Rovelli, *The Order of Time*, p. 44.
4 Rovelli, *The Order of Time*, p. 51.
5 Jorge Luis Borges, *Labyrinths*. New York: New Directions, 2007, p. 221.
6 St Augustine and Henry Chadwick. *Confessions*. Oxford: Oxford University Press, 1991, p. 241.
7 St Augustine, *The Confessions*, p. 242.
8 Rovelli, *The Order of Time*, p. 184.
9 St. Augustine, *The Confessions*, p. 240.
10 Email with the Author, October 2024.
11 Email with the Author, October 2024.
12 Email with the Author, October 2024.
13 Unknown source often wrongly attributed to Lewis Carroll's *Alice's Adventures in Wonderland*.
14 Email with the Author, October 2024.
15 Email with the Author, October 2024.
16 Email with the Author, October 2024.
17 Rovelli, *The Order of Time*, p. 91.
18 Rovelli, *The Order of Time*, p. 91.
19 Rovelli, *The Order of Time*, p. 91.
20 Mark McElhatten, *Views From the Avante Garde*, 2008 NY Film Festival.
21 Email with the Author, October 2024.

BIBLIOGRAPHY

Armstrong, Karen, *A Short History of Myth*. Edinburgh: Canongate Books Ltd, 2005.

Barthes, Roland, *A Lover's Discourse*. New York: Hill and Wang, 2010.

Barthes, Roland, *Mythologies*. New York: Hill and Wang, 2013.

Debord, Guy, *The Society of the Spectacle*. Paris: Critical Editions, 2021.

Fromm, Erich, *The Art of Loving*. New York: Harper Perennial Modern Classics, 2019.

Kierkegaard, Soren, *Works of Love*. New York: Harper Perennial, 2009.

Plato, *The Republic and Other Works*. New York: Anchor Books, 1973.

Plato, *The Symposium*. London: Penguin Classics, 1999.

Robinson, Chris, *Earmarked for Collision: A Highly Biased Tour of Collage Animation*. Boca Raton: CRC Press, 2023.

Rovelli, Carlo, *The Order of Time*. New York: Riverhead Books, 2018.

Sontag, Susan, *Against Interpretation and Other Essays*. New York: Picador, 1966.

Sontag, Susan, *On Photography*. London: Penguin Books, 2019.

Sontag, Susan, *Regarding the Pain of Others*. New York: Picador, 2003.

Woodworth, Mark, *Bee Thousand*. New York: Continuum Press, 2011.

Lewis Klahr: Selected Filmography

SUPER 8 AND 16MM

Picture Books for Adults 1983–1985 8 films 34:44 Super 8 sound B&W and color
Deep Fishtank Birding 1983 2:58
Enchantment 1983 3:22
Pulls 1985 3:30
What's Going On Here, Joe? 1984 4:12
The River Sieve 1985 4:42
Candee's 16! 1984 3:02
Deep Fishtank Too 1985 4:24
1966 1984 8:34
Her Fragrant Emulsion 1987 10:36 16mm color sound
Blown up from Super 8
Tales of the Forgotten Future 1988–1991 12 films 135:46
Super 8 B&W Color Sound & Silent
Part One: The Morning Films 33:44 B&W, sound
Lost Camel Intentions 1988 10:09
For the Rest of Your Natural Life 1988 8:38
In the Month of Crickets 1988 14:57
Part Two: Five O'clock Worlds 28:27 Color, Sound
The Organ Minder's Gronkey 1990 14:53
Hi-Fi Cadets 1989 11:16
Verdant Sonar 1990 2:18
Part Three: Mood Opulence 34:04 Sound
Cartoon Far 1990 6:08 color
Yesterday's Glue 1990 14:16 B&W
Elevator Music 1991 13:40 color
Part Four: Right Hand Shade 38:23 Silent
Station Drama 1990 13:35 B&W
The Life of Naomi Lang 1991 20:49 B&W and Color
Actuality 1991 3:59 B&W
Engram Sepals
(Melodramas 1993–2000) 16mm 81:27 color & B&W sound

Altair 1995 8min.
Engram Sepals 2000 6:22
Elsa Kirk 1999 5:16
Pony Glass 1997 14:50
Govinda 1999 23:33
Downs Are Feminine 1993 9:54
A Failed Cardigan Maneuver 1999 13:32
The Aperture of Ghostings (1999–2001) 13:05 16mm color sound
Elsa Kirk 1999 5:18
Catherine Street 2001 3:11
Creased Robe Smile 2001 4:36
Daylight Moon (A Quartet) 2002–2004 41:21 16mm sound color
Valise 2004 15:18
Hard Green 2004 5:10
Soft Ticket 2004 7:42
Daylight Moon 2002 13:11
The Two Minutes to Zero Trilogy 2003–2004 32:13 16mm color sound
Two Days to Zero 2004 22:35
Two Hours to Zero 2004 8:32
Music by Rhys Chatham "Guitar Trio"
Two Minutes to Zero 2003 1:06
Music by Glenn Branca an excerpt from "The Ascension"
Take Me Tonight 1985 3m super 8 color sound
The Nightengale's Fisted Wave-- 1985 blow up super 8 to 16mm
City Film super 8 1992 17min. color silent Transfer to Digital Video 2013
The Pharaoh's Belt 1994 43min. color, sound 16mm
Music by Last Forever
Whirligigs in the Late Afternoon 1996 25min. color silent 16mm
Lulu 1996 3:24 color sound 16mm
Green '62 1996 6min. silent color
The Speed of Turquoise 1995 23m color sound 16mm
Calendar the Siamese 1997 30min. color, sound 16mm
Marietta's Lied 1998 5:05 color sound 16mm
A House Is Not a Home (co-directed with Travis Preston)
B&W Silent 2004 15min. 16mm

DIGITAL VIDEO

Antigenic Drift 2007 17min. Color Sound
Music by Rhys Chatham
The Diptherians: Episode Two—The Rhythm That Forgets Itself
2008 14:45 Color Sound with Kate Valk, Willem Dafoe, and Henry Stram Music by Tom Recchion
Well Then There Now 13:30 2011 script and music John Zorn

Narration Slater Klahr
Prolix Satori (an ongoing open ended series, 2009–to the Present)
False Aging (14:45 2008) Color Sound
The Couplets
April Snow (2010 10min)
A Thousand Julys (6:30 2010)
Nimbus Smile (8:30 2009)
Nimbus Seeds (8:30 2009)
Cumulonimbus (9:30 2010)
Sugar Slim Says (8m 2010)
Wednesday Morning Two A.M. 6:30 2009
The Rain Couplets (2012 14:30)
Kiss The Rain 2012 6m & **The Street of Everlasting Rain** 2012 8:30
The Pettifogger (2011 65min)
Sixty-Six 12 Films (2002–2015) 90:00
(Projection order with Episode Numbers)
1.
Episode 11, **Mercury** (3m 2015)
2.
Episode One, **Ichor** (5m 2013)
Music: Mark Anthony Thompson Narration: Andrea Leblanc
3.
Episode Three, **Helen of T** (7m, 2013)
4.
Episode 4, **Erigone's Daughter** (15m 2014)
Original Music by Josh Rosen, performed by 3 Play
5.
Episode Five, **Mars Garden** (5m 2014)
6.
Episode 6, **Saturn's Diary** (6:45 2014)
7.
Episode Ten, **The Silver Age** (9m 2015)
8.
Episode Eight, **August 19, 1966 (Jupiter Sends A Message)** (5m 2014)
9.
Episode Nine, **Lip Print (Venus)** (3m 2012)
10.
Episode Seven, **Ambrosia** (4:30 2014)
11.
Episode Two, **Orphacles** (5m, 2013)
Original music Mark Anthony Thompson, Narration Andrea Leblanc
12.
Episode Twelve, **Lethe** (21:30 2010)
Various Titles not included in Prolix Satori
Album (2012 33m)
Mercury (2009 55seconds)
L.A. (2011 3:20) Music by Gabriel Kahane

Turn It Back (2012 2:45) created for Chuck Workman's Doc What Is Cinema? And used as an excerpt and included in its full cut as an extra on the DVD release. Retitled as **Lip Print (Venus)** and included in **Sixty-Six** as the 9th episode and 9th film in the projection order.

The Moon Has Its Reasons 2012 3m Commissioned by Channel 4 UK

Open Eye Sleep 2012 2:45 with Henry Stram, Kate Valk, Willem Dafoe, Daniel Zippi, Kevin O'Brian Music Tom Recchion

Color Diary (Sketch) 2:25 2013

The Occidental Hotel 26m 2014

Serrated Edge (12:58 July 2015) formerly the first version of Circumstantial Pleasures re-titled for premier screening in Berwick Festival Fall 2015 curated by Peter Taylor

Circumstantial Pleasures (15:13 July 2016) the second version of this film which premiered in my solo show "Circumstantial Pleasures" at Grieder Contemporary, Zurich September–October 2016

High Rise (1:51 September 2017) video component of 2-D collage "Streets" exhibited in my solo show "Circumstantial Pleasures" at Grieder Contemporary, Zurich September–October 2016

Ratchet The Margin (6:45 November 2016) [briefly the third version of Circumstantial Pleasures but never exhibited before name change]

Part of in-progress series: *Circumstantial* Pleasures

Capitalist Roaders (17:58 December 2016)

Part of in-progress series: *Circumstantial Pleasures*

D.B.S. (7:19 February 2017)

Music by Royal Auditorium their song S.B.S.

Black River Falls (6:30 June 2017)

Music by Dick Connette from his album Too Sad for the Public Vol. 1: Oysters Ice Cream Lemonade

Out of Truth (Don't Motto) (10m April 2018)

Music David Rosenboom

Dead Celebrity (4:30 June 2018)

Music– Ex Mykah (Bryan Senti)

Virulent Capital (8m, June 2018) version 1

music David Rosenboom: Music for Analog Computers (1968–1969)

Hammond Song (5:30m August 2018)

Music- The Roches

Circumstantial Pleasures (2013–2020, 65m)

Capitalist Roaders (2016, 18m music: David Rosenboom, Tom Recchion

Ramification Lesions (Microbial Stress) (2019, 7m music: David Rosenboom

Rachet the Margin (2016, 6:32); music: Tom Recchion

Virulent Capital (2018, 9m) music: David Rosenboom

High Rise (2016, 3m)

Circumstantial Pleasures (2019, 22m); music: Scott Walker

The Blue Rose of Forgetfulness (2021, 63:30)

Monogram (2019, 9m)

Swollen Kisses (2019, 6m)

Capitulations Promise (2020, 6:34)

Blue Sun (2020, 14m)

Alcestis (2021, 22m)
The Blue Rose of Forgetfulness (2020, 5:18)
Five Days Till Tomorrow (2022, 13:21)
Railroad Bill (2023, 6:33)
Interstitial Romance (Warm Novelette) (2024, 6m)
Thin Rain (2023, 15:24)
The Plash of Fountains (2024, 19:19)
Repast (2024, 4m)
Three Friends of the Cold Season (2024, 14:40)

Index

Note: *Italic* page numbers refer to figures and page numbers followed by "n" denote endnotes.

For Product Safety Concerns and Information please contact our EU representative GPSR@taylorandfrancis.com
Taylor & Francis Verlag GmbH, Kaufingerstraße 24, 80331 München, Germany

www.ingramcontent.com/pod-product-compliance
Lightning Source LLC
LaVergne TN
LVHW010931110826
845149LV00013B/2552

* 9 7 8 1 0 3 2 5 4 7 2 9 9 *